The
Debateable
Land

The Debateable Land

Ireland's border counties

Edited by
Brian S Turner

Published by The Ulster Local History Trust
in association with The Heritage Council
2002

Designed by Barry Craig
Printed by W&G Baird

ISBN 0 9542832 0 1

Photographs:
John Bradley; pp 56 & 58
Bobbie Hanvey; p 19
Reg Hill; back cover and pp 6, 8, 72, 89,
    90 & 91
Northern Standard; p 10
Edward O'Kane; pp 60, 61 & 62
Allen Thompson, Down County Museum;
    pp 41, 42 & 43
Brian Turner; cover and pp 46, 47 & 48
Aidan Walsh; pp 31, 34, 35 & 36

Front cover illustration:
*Monea Castle, County Fermanagh, built
for Malcolm Hamilton in 1618.*

Ulster Local History Trust
Box 900
Downpatrick
County Down BT30 6EF

Back cover:
*Communication: Pauric Clerkin of
Monaghan County Museum and Seamus
Heaney.*

Contents

Promoting community identity, locality, and mumming.

Preface

To have tension, boundaries, contradictions at your heart can be painful and unsettling, but it may also stimulate creativity. From Ireland's border counties people look north, south, east, and west, and for those who live there they are, and ought to be, the centre of the world. And within the border counties can be found the greatest variety of social and economic, religious and political traditions of the island. It is, perhaps, no accident that within the troubled second half of the twentieth century this is an area, on both sides of the political boundary, which has led the way both in the formation of voluntary local historical societies and in the establishment of publicly funded county museums.

It was with this in mind that the Ulster Local History Trust approached the idea of the conference recorded in this book. It was entitled *The Debateable Land: Ireland's border counties* and was organised for local historians by the Ulster Local History Trust in partnership with the Heritage Council. It took place in the Lakeside Hotel, Monaghan, on 16th and 17th November 2001.

The conference heard four main addresses, spaced over two days, by Seamus Heaney, Patrick Duffy, John Lynch, and Myrtle Hill, whose contributions were carefully planned both to locate our interest in a human framework and to provide practical advice to local historians. No less important was the decision to invite a variety of practitioners to give shorter presentations on a variety of topics which allowed more voices to illustrate the energy of the local history movement. This energy too was represented by the wealth of publications for sale, the music and song of David Hammond and Neil Martin, the exhibition from Monaghan County Museum, the presentation of certificates for the National University of Ireland's Maynooth course in local history, taught in Blacklion, County Cavan. The noise and music, dance and fun of the Aughakillymaude Mummers from Fermanagh left straw on the carpet as a reminder of their vigorous contribution and a very appropriate ingredient in the mixture. The 180 participants in the conference came from twenty of Ireland's counties and constituted what was probably the largest ever gathering of local historians in the border counties.

We are most grateful to our partners, the Heritage Council, for their generous financial and moral support for this venture. Three members of the Council, Dr Patricia Donlon, Mr Michael MacMahon and Professor William Smyth not only chaired sessions but contributed in other ways from their own experience, and Beatrice Kelly, the Council's Education Officer, acted as helpful liaison throughout. Monaghan County Council were generous with hospitality. The Ulster Local History Trust is a small voluntary body and particular acknowledgement is due to those trustees who formed the organising committee for the conference; Doreen Corcoran, Jack Johnston, Brian Turner, Myrtle Hill and Theo MacMahon. Marie O'Neill and Michelle McGoff in Monaghan coped magnificently with the traumas of managing conference registration in Ireland.

Students presented at the conference with certificates in Local History from the National University of Ireland, Maynooth. The course, involving lectures and a dissertation, was taught at Blacklion, County Cavan, and hosted by the Border Counties History Collective.
Left to right: Dr Raymond Gillespie (NUI, Maynooth), Jack Johnston (Course Director), Maureen Keaney, Brian Curran, Pat O'Brien, Dr Jacinta Prunty (NUI, Maynooth), Marianna Maguire, Seosamh Ó Luana, Grace McGuinness, Larry Mullin, George Knight, Eileen Kelly, Sean McGauran, and Prin Duignan (Tutor).

Foreword

Driving north to Monaghan on a dark, rainy November day to attend a joint Heritage Council/Ulster Local History Trust weekend conference on 'The Debatable Land' I felt some anticipation but mostly a sense of duty. Nothing, however, could have prepared me for the sheer energy, enthusiasm and commitment of the participants, and thus a weekend that began as a duty quickly changed to one of absorption and enlightenment. Speakers from the poetic and inspirational Seamus Heaney to the pragmatic John Lynch held their audiences captive over the almost two day conference, each speaker telling their personal stories, drawing us back in time, whilst rooting us firmly in the landscape of today, and in particular that complex stretch of land known as the borderlands.

The geographical reality, the political line between two states, furnished us with stories of an older border, with Aidan Walsh walking us through his excavations of 'The Black Pig's Dyke'. We heard of the differing iconographies of what Patrick J Duffy called "the windows on both states". We listened to stories of smugglers and to poems and songs that immortalized those smugglers. There was religion too – How could there not be? – but not in any tired manner but rather in an example of how museums through their exhibitions show not just the past, but can be a positive force for change in the present. As Brian Turner reminded us, "We all know that history is about today rather than yesterday." The humanity and understanding of the various scholars, researchers and participants and the sensitivity with which they tackled their individual projects was remarkable. One of the speakers later reinforced this when Myrtle Hill urged us to remember that having researched our projects "any conclusions reached must reflect the complexities of human experience." Through each of the wide-ranging papers was the reality of human experience and the echoes of those idiosyncratic, sometimes funny, often painfully personal voices of the inhabitants of the borderlands, rescued from oblivion through patient research.

That then was what was on offer from the podium from a fascinating team of expert players, but what of the other participants? Pragmatism and poetry mingled on the ground too, with tables laden with local history publications under siege from a bevy of eager buyers, the clink of coffee cups sounding against the background swell of chat and charm with soft voices murmuring apologetically "I'm just an amateur", forgetting that therein lies the power and endurance of local history studies on this island. The etymology of amateur is from the Latin amatorum – 'a lover of something'. No amount of 'book learning' can ever challenge the true amateur as was clearly and demonstrably shown during 'The Debatable Land' conference.

The Heritage Council is committed to several key aims over its current term of office, amongst them raising awareness and appreciation of our heritage and placing it at the heart of public life. These papers celebrate a weekend which is a perfect example of how those aims can become a pleasurable and profitable reality. Let us continue to meet, talk and debate, whilst researching and documenting the many varying facets of this frustrating, fascinating land of ours. Let us continue to do it through a partnership of like minds and perhaps make the event recorded in these pages a regular feature on the calendar.

Dr Pat Donlon
Chair of the Education and Awareness Committee
Heritage Council

Spring 2002

Seamus Heaney and Jack Johnston.

Keeping the accent

Seamus Heaney

It's impossible for a poet to come to Monaghan and not think of Patrick Kavanagh, and since Kavanagh has written one of the definitive border-dispute poems, I want to begin with him. Familiar as the poem is, it always bears repeating. It's about that epic row concerning the march between the Duffys' land and the McCabes', during the year of the Munich Crisis, in 1938. But crisis in Munich becomes 'bother' in Monaghan, as Kavanagh sets the annexation of Czechoslovakia by Germany in the scales against the appropriation of a right-of-way in the parish of Inniskeen.

I have lived in important places, times
When great events were decided. Who owned
That half a rood of rock, a no-man's land
Surrounded by our pitch-fork armed claims.
I heard the Duffys shouting 'Damn your soul'
And old McCabe, stripped to the waist, seen
Step the plot, denying blue cast-steel --
'Here is the march along these iron stones.'
That was the year of the Munich bother. Which
Was more important? I inclined
To lose my faith in Ballyrush and Gortin
Till Homer's ghost came whispering to my mind
He said: I made the *Illiad* from such
A local row. Gods make their own importance.

Kavanagh is concerned with the Duffys and the McCabes, all right, but he is even more concerned with getting a poem out of them. Like any artist, he's interested in what can be made of his subject matter. Reporting a story is one thing. The *Dundalk Democrat* or the *Impartial Reporter* can do that, and indeed the columns of country newspapers used to be full of accounts of litigation between small farmers over rights of way. In fact, when people used to assemble on their *ceilidhe* in our own kitchen in County Derry in the nineteen forties, the talk would sooner or later turn into a rehearsal of arguments used in old court cases about who had which right of access to what cart-road or kesh or loaning.

Still, as I say, it's one thing to present the facts. Making something of them, artistically and imaginatively, is something else, and that is the challenge the writer faces, whether the subject be the border between two jurisdictions in Ireland or the disputed ground between two farms in Inniskeen.

What Kavanagh makes of it is a parable about the way the local can be valued and embraced as a counterbalance to a value-system based on some larger national or international consensus.

And one of the ways he manages to do this, of course, is by keeping the local accent. "Damn your soul" - or is it 'sowl' rhyming with 'howl'? However it's pronounced, it was never part of the received language of poetry; it belongs on the lips of the people. And so does the word 'march' meaning the boundary, and the Munich 'bother': by adding those small units of Monaghan usage to the local side of the linguistic scales, Kavanagh tilts the balance, disturbs the consensus and demands, as it were, a recount.

Kavanagh always had his feet on the ground but, in spite of his down-to-earthness, he would end up convinced that it was often best to do what Tyrone Guthrie, another great border artist, used to advise his friends to do in adversity. "Rise above", was Guthrie's motto, and Kavanagh ultimately developed a way of regarding things from a Parnassian perspective, even if his local hill of poetry was the Big Forth in Rocksavage rather than a big mountain in Greece. In his final view any manifestation of social concern, political engagement, or civic purpose vitiated the poet's purpose. Reading him, you have a wonderful sense of a free spirit rising to the occasion. Rising above but at the same time not deserting the facts. And it is that combination of a broad horizon of understanding with an intimate fidelity to what's near at hand, the combination of the view from Parnassus with the view from the parish, it is that which is finally exemplary about his work.

The broad horizon cannot be scorned. The elevation of Ballyrush and Gortin is a countermeasure, a corrective tactic, a call to people not to get beyond themselves, as it were, not to become part of the masses who consume the media message and sway like crops in the global breeze. But Ballyrush and Gortin are not the final reality either. As Kavanagh himself said, advising people to be proud of their parish is not without its dangers; when, for example, he calls the places he has lived in "important places" and calls the Munich crisis "bother", he does so with a certain self-consciousness; he knows what he is doing; he is aware that he is transgressing and upsetting the applecart of the conventional; he's exhibiting an enlightened contrariness rather than a blinkered ignorance. There is always, therefore, a saving irony in his refusal to acknowledge the perspectives of the larger world.

Kavanagh keeps faithful to the local by keeping the local accent. "The bicycles go by in twos and threes" on the Inniskeen Road. They do not pass by, as they might in a more cosmopolitan setting, nor do they go past; the Duffys are shouting, "Damn your soul"; the cattle drovers in Shancoduff are asking "Who owns them hungry hills?" – never 'those' hungry hills. Which is to say that the vocabulary and the cadence in his poems are what he would have heard in his parish: just take this stanza at random from 'Art McCooey'.

"I'll see you after second Mass on Sunday."

"Right-o, right-o." The mare moves on again.

A wheel rides over a heap of gravel

And the mare goes skew-ways like a blinded hen.

What is worth noticing here is the way Kavanagh's lines keep the accent in two different senses. "I heard the Duffys shouting, Damn your soul." "Here is the march along these iron stones." "The bicycles go by in twos and threes." "'Right-o, right-o'. The mare moves on again." These lines are certainly lines you could hear spoken in Monaghan, but they are also natural iambic pentameters. The accent falls where the pattern of the metre requires it. They are in step with Shakespeare's "When I do count the clock that tells the time" and Thomas Gray's "The curfew tolls the knell of parting day." Kavanagh has an ear for border speech, all right, an ear to the local ground; but inside that ear there is a listening post that picks up other messages. There are surveillance devices in it that receive signals from poetry stations on the broader horizon. The author knows about Wilfred Owen in Flanders as well as Hector in Troy. He knows about the new technique that Owen developed, the device known as half- or pararhyme. Look at *Epic* again, for example, and hear the sophisticated, artfully underplayed half-rhymes: 'times' and 'claims', 'owned' and 'land', 'soul' and 'steel', 'which' and 'such', 'inclined' and 'mind', and finally, suiting the rhyme to the theme, 'Gortin' and 'importance'.

So, for all of Kavanagh's insistence on the centrality of Ballyrush and Gortin, the poem also reveals how much his own understanding of this centrality depends on a knowledge of a wider world. He has travelled in the realms of gold as well as in the loanings of Inniskeen; he knows about sonnets as well as about sheughs; he knows about the anger of Achilles as well as the rage of Old McCabe. Kavanagh in effect lives between understandings and idioms, as we all do. In order to keep the accent in the fullest sense, we have to keep the lines open to all the different terminuses, or termini, of consciousness. If we shut down communications with what is coming in to us, we are shutting down on our full humanity.

* * * * *

Our understanding is at once structured by boundaries and impatient of them. We have a capacity to see from above how limiting they are and at the same time an inclination to stand by them and thereby stand our ground. My favourite image of this is something I read concerning the temple of Jupiter in ancient Rome. Apparently in Jupiter's temple there was an image of another god as well, the one the Romans called Terminus, the god of boundaries. And what was interesting and odd and paradoxical was the fact that the image of Terminus was placed in a part of the temple that was open to the sky, as if to indicate that there were indeed two ways of understanding the boundary itself; on the one hand, common sense recognized it as an earthly necessity, a given of the terrestrial estate; and on the other, the imagination conceived of it as a barrier, a limit set to the desire for boundlessness that is built into us all.

The theme of the border, in other words, has a meaning that opens inwards and outwards. It acknowledges that contradiction is a condition that we may deplore and yet have to endure. It asks you to square the circle, to keep your feet on the ground and your head in the air at the same time, to be honest to earth and honest to God. And yet human beings have the capacity to live with contradiction. They are creative intelligences and can always make something of the conditions they are landed into.

* * * * *

What needs to be emphasized, I suppose, is the fact that living on a border, be it a topographical or cultural or literary or linguistic one, gives opportunities for crossovers as well as stand-offs. In that one poem of Kavanagh's, there's enough linguistic, literary and cultural complexity to keep us going for the rest of the evening. You could begin by thinking of the history of the term 'no-mans land', for example, and consider how it translates from Flanders fields to the fields of the Irish Free State. Or you could ponder the use of the word 'march' and realize that as well as delineating the boundary between two farms of land, it opens across to the marches between England and Wales. To put it another way, you begin to realize that while Kavanagh lives in a topography where the placenames constitute what John Montague once called 'a primal Gaeltacht', he uses an idiom that bespeaks what we might call 'a parish Galltacht'. The main thing is to realize that the more we keep burrowing down the more things keep opening up.

I myself, for example, am keen on taking the word 'march' as far as it can be taken. It's a word I used to hear again and again in those conversations about rights of way, and in other farming contexts. It was not then automatically associated in my ear with Drumcree and Ormeau Road, with protest marches and marching seasons. There were marching days all right, the twelfth of July and the twelfth of August, the seventeenth of March and the fifteenth of August, but in the first world I knew the marching season as such was every season in the year, because it was the land itself that did the marching. The verb meant to meet a boundary, to be bordered by, to be matched up to yet to be marked off from. One farm marched another farm; one field marched another field; and what divided them, as in the case of the McCabes and Duffys, was the march drain or the march hedge.

In that first usage, the word did not mean "to walk in a military manner", but to be close, to lie alongside, to border and be bordered upon. It was a word that suggested division but contained also a definite suggestion of solidarity. If my land marched your land, we were bound by that boundary as well as separated by it. If the whole of the liberating sky was over the head of the god Terminus, the whole of the solid earth was under what he stood for, the march hedge and the march drain. And what this meditation on the word teaches me could be expressed in the words of the seventeenth century Japanese poet Bashō:

> What is important [Bashō wrote] is to keep our mind high in the world of true understanding, and returning to the world of our daily experience, to seek

therein the truth of beauty. No matter what we may be doing at any given moment, we must not forget that it has a bearing upon our everlasting self which is poetry.

Bashō makes the mind sound a bit like that Roman image of Terminus, earthbound and present in the here and now, yet open to what he calls in his Zen-like way "the everlasting self", the boundlessness of inner as well as outer space. Indeed, he sounds a bit like Tyrone Guthrie counselling us to "rise above".

To follow a word like march to its source is not a matter of narrowing down a meaning but of opening up a horizon, changing the plane of regard. One of the best things we could do nowadays is to put our ears to the ground of our own first speech, the spoken language, that is, of Ulster. All of its underground passages and galleries, its old forgotten mineshafts of myth and memory, are still there to be explored. There are blind alleys down there which we have to turn into escape hatches. We have to get the system on the move and breathing again. Get the dead air of ethnic solidarity and identity politics circulating. Get a wind of change blowing through.

The fencing off of Planter from Gael, the concern with separate heritages, the need to trace an ancestry and establish a birthright, the authority and freedom to say, "Here is the march along these iron stones" - all of that constitutes a first stage, something to build on, something that makes available to us the community ore from which a self can be fashioned; this should, however, be a beginning rather than an end in itself. Good fences may indeed make good neighbours, but even so, the first line of Robert Frost's famous poem about mending fences says "Something there is that does not love a wall." Come to think of it, the paradox of boundaries is also revealed by that phrase I've just used: "mending fences" should logically put us in mind of barriers being reinstated and exclusive premises being re-established, but oddly enough the human import of the phrase is exactly the opposite. When we mend fences, we mean that relationships can open again, certain barriers can be taken down and comings and goings can recommence between your house and my house.

What I am saying is that keeping the accent can be a creative rather than a contrary exercise. It can be as much a matter of shifting the ground as of standing it. The accent, in other words, is one of our talents and we need to be a good steward to it. It's natural enough to want to keep what we have inherited and to cherish the good of it, but we need to try to conceive of the future by meditating on that heritage; and meditating on our linguistic heritage in particular (as I hope I have shown in the case of 'march') is potentially a liberating activity.

* * * * *

'The other', for example, is a central concept in contemporary theories of identity building. Thinking in binary terms, imagining the opposite is a necessary part of that operation: in order to be 'us' we need a 'them'; in order to be Irish we need an English, in order to be Protestant we need a Catholic, and so on. In a land where 'the other side' and 'the other sort' are a constant part of the vernacular, we require very little theoretical instruction on that point. Nevertheless, in post-colonial thinking and in current academic discourse, this notion of 'the other' remains a dominant and productive intellectual device.

I would like, therefore, to propose a development of the concept. At this conference about the borderlands, being held in the borderlands, I suggest that we should consider the virtues and rewards of 'the through-other'. You remember W F Marshall's explanation of how a row got settled in Tyrone:

That and all, we got great before morning.

We were friends through other, you see.

I don't mean to invoke 'through-otherness' as a folksy evasion of the political, social and sectarian realities of life in Ulster, north of the border, on the border, south of the border. What I want to do, rather, is to use a word and a concept that is familiar to us in the world of our daily experience and to ponder it in the light of what Bashō called "the world of true understanding." I seriously mean that it can be made to rise above itself.

There is a through-otherness, in the colloquial sense, about the way we live with the divisions among us - all you need to do is to think of the carry-on in and around the Stormont Assembly; but the term can be re-focused, turned into a future-seeking device, so to speak. We can think of it as an encouragement to cross the line, to move out over no-man's land into each other's trenches, to start that flow I was talking about earlier, turn the blind alley of 'us' and 'them' into the escape route of becoming friends through other, and thereby becoming, in all senses, great. 'Great', as generations of Scullions and Heaneys were great with generations of Junkins, on both sides of the march drain; but great also in spirit and in vision, as we are called upon to be and need to be in years to come.

I'd therefore like to end by reading two pieces of my own poetry. First, the conclusion to a poem called 'The Other Side' which could have equally well been called 'The Other Sort'. In this final section, the Presbyterian neighbour lands on his *ceilidhe* when the Catholic family are on their knees in the kitchen, at their prayers:

Then sometimes when the rosary was dragging
mournfully on in the kitchen
we would hear his step round the gable

though not until after the litany
would the knock come to the door
and the casual whistle strike up

on the doorstep. 'A right looking night,'
he might say, 'I was dandering by and says I,
I might as well call.'

But now I stand behind him
in the dark yard, in the moan of prayers.
He puts a hand in a pocket

or taps a little tune with the blackthorn
shyly, as if he were party to
lovemaking or a stranger's weeping.

Should I slip away, I wonder,
or go up and touch his shoulder
and talk about the weather

or the price of grass-seed?

Talking about the weather or the price of grass-seed can be an evasion of
difference, but it can equally well be the start of an attempt to bridge it. And in
a similar fashion, keeping the accent can be symptomatic of a reductive,
defensive smallness of attitude or it can bespeak a confidence and inner
freedom that opens the way to magnanimity. So in conclusion I'll read a poem
that celebrates the local as a source of healing and refreshment and conceives of
the local accent as a redemptive resource rather than regressive symptom

It's called 'The Guttural Muse' and I wrote it in the late 1970s, after I had
spent a week on location with a film crew in County Monaghan. We were doing
a TV programme on Patrick Kavanagh and had made our base in the Nuremore
Hotel outside Carrickmacross. One night there, late and tired, I headed up the
stairs for bed, but was suddenly aware that down under me in the hotel, a disco
was in full swing, so I thought, "That's that", and gave up any hope of getting
to sleep. Still, it was the summertime and I was happy to drift in pensive mood
over to the open window and take it easy, inhaling the coolth and the country
air. And as I sat listening to the decibels of the disco I began, of course, to think
conventional thoughts about the erosion of local life, about the invasion of the
townland by the transistor, about the way globalization was rocking and rolling
the come-all-ye singer out of his corner, about the end of an era in Ireland, and
everywhere else, for that matter. And as I drifted in this haze of received ideas
the crowd began to pour out of the disco and suddenly I was listening to the
ram-stam and hullabulloo of Monaghan accents in full cry. And any
wistfulness I felt was quickly overcome. The mood of elegy evaporated. As I
listened to those gowls and hoaghs and yelps and cat-calls, I knew there was
something undaunted and resistant about them. They were unreconstructed
and fit for anybody or anything.

In the poem I wrote later, I alluded to an old folk belief about the tench fish
and used it as a metaphor for the hale and healing power of dialect and the

local accent. The tench, a bottom-feeder, a slimy old bubbler under the lily pads, was once called 'the doctor fish' because people believed his slime had the power to cure wounds of other fish that had been scored by the gaff, perhaps, or torn by a hook. I would like to believe that in the guttural accents that underlie our standardized speech, in the capacity we have for bringing forth new meanings from the old vernacular, there is a corresponding curative power, a promise of new growth and second life; and more generally I would suggest that it is the heaviness of this local, guttural accent that will save us from the weightlessness of the global babble that everywhere surrounds us:

> Late summer, and at midnight
> I smelt the heat of the day:
> At my window over the hotel car park
> I breathed the muddied night airs off the lake
> And watched a young crowd leave the discotheque.
>
> Their voices rose up thick and comforting
> As oily bubbles the feeding tench sent up
> That evening at dusk - the slimy tench
> Once called the 'doctor fish' because his slime
> Was said to heal the wounds of fish that touched it.
>
> A girl in a white dress
> Was being courted out among the cars:
> As her voice swarmed and puddled into laughs
> I felt like some old pike, all badged with sores,
> Wanting to swim in touch with soft-mouthed life.

Acknowledgement

Patrick Kavanagh's *Epic* is reprinted by permission of the trustees of the estate of the late Katherine B Kavanagh, through the Jonathan Williams Literary Agency.

David Hammond, film-maker, folklorist, broadcaster, and singer, and Neil Martin, film-maker, composer , and versatile instrumentalist, both entertained and added substance to the subject of the conference with a performance entitled 'A hinterland to the border'.

Continuity and change in the Border landscapes

Patrick J Duffy

> I told him the route I had taken and asked if it was possible that I had come from the North into the South, into the North again, and into the South once more without a single signpost or checkpoint, without a significant change in the look of the landscape or the quality of the road…. He laughed. It was possible, yes.[1]

Introduction

As a place, as a landscape, the borderlands have had a more or less higher or lower profile over the decades since they were formally instituted in 1920-22. Although today as a result of European Union initiatives and other political changes, not least the 'Good Friday Agreement', the border itself has less social and economic significance, its landscapes endure. The 'troubles' of the past thirty years, however, confounded most moves to closer European regional integration in the area[2] and only served to consolidate the borderlands as a separate militarised region, with its by-roads and minor bridges blocked or broken. The border also featured prominently during recent agricultural crises - BSE and foot-and-mouth disease - when this boundary between the United Kingdom and the Irish Republic took on a strategic significance that should bewilder apologists for both loyalism and republicanism. Northern Irish cattle were characterised as 'British' by Joe Walsh, the agriculture minister in Dublin, and 'Irish' by Ian Paisley in Brussels.

David Harkness has claimed that the border was not that important – in terms of leisure, holidays, cultural and, increasingly, economic activities it is ignored.[3] Nevertheless one's experience suggests otherwise: few undergraduate students from south Leinster or Munster would be familiar with Northern Ireland, and how many loyalists from Shankill or Portadown are familiar with the Republic?

Representations of border landscapes

There are approximately 800,000 people living in the borderlands, one tenth of the population of the Republic and more than a quarter of the population of Northern Ireland. From a distance the border is a simple geographical reality – a political line in a landscape crossed by south-to-north highways linking two states.[4] From close up, it is a complex labyrinth of roads, lanes and tracks, streams and hedgerows intertwining round local lives.

There is, firstly, the big picture from Dublin, or Belfast or London, where the border has represented the official meeting place of administrations. This is the top-down view from the centres, where 'sovereignty' was jealousy guarded. Here was a deliberately maintained and constructed ideological view, where the nuanced symbolism of each side's perspective was most visible. I remember occasional official 'diplomatic' protests in the past being delivered by the Irish government about incursions over the border by British security forces, and the symbolism of signposting by both states or local authorities: the assertive bilingualism in the southern borders - Derry/Doire; 'Fáilte go Muineacháin – and the pointed British-standard signposts to Londonderry in the north; Britain's modern 'Give way' signs versus the Republic's more obsolete 'Yield right of way'! The borderlands were the windows on both states, where particular displays of the iconography of nationhood were most obvious, and where they have both worked diligently since partition at engineering their individual distinctiveness.[5]

All of this was complicated by the fact that, in theory, the South wanted to ignore the border's existence but in fact had to deal with it on a day-to-day basis. Recent work on state papers shows that De Valera, in spite of public pronouncements to the contrary, accepted it much more than was thought.[6] I recall the first time I looked at the Irish Census of Population in the 1960s and discovered that I belonged to a place called 'Ulster (part of)'. For someone from Monaghan there was something sad about this description – a sense of loss, incompleteness, or a disenfranchisement of identity. Though it might appear that Northern Ireland did not have this problem, because it was the uncomplicated remaining, and bigger, part of Ulster, Sean Ó Faoláin sixty years ago equally considered that 'The Six Counties' was an unlovely name "because there is no such place... How can she have pride in it with a digital name and a partitioned land."[7] As administrative realities, of course, the six counties were abolished in the 1970s, to be replaced by more modern districts. Although there were selective references in the north to 'the people of Ulster' for almost a century, it was a term which was not inclusive of the majority in the historic lands of Ulster. There is, therefore, an enduring contestation, a crisis of placelessness, which is especially pronounced in the borderlands and which is a product of diverging ideological stances by the states. A geographically confused American was prophetic in his assessment of the border's role at the dawn of its existence.

> The Irish Border has been like a dragon squatting between the Free State and Ulster, threatening to consume them both. It thrives on complexities. It has devoured any number of speeches, debates, conferences, and judicial committees... [8]

Such constructed disconnection is manifest in Seamus Heaney's memory of the emblematic thick red line around Northern Ireland on his primary school wall map, with the dotted ferry lines emphasising umbilical links with Scotland and England, turning away from the rest of the island, like the history books which also turned their backs on the island's past.[9] Meanwhile the Free State's earlier maps often showed the island of Ireland with no border, and its children were deeply imbued with the island's history, especially as it helped to explain the genesis of the borderland.

The borderlands continue, of course, to be marked with the symbols of these enduring national contestations on what are effectively the militarised peripheries of both states: the UDA flag-bedecked crossroads of north Armagh and the IRA monuments of south Armagh. From many a northern unionist perspective, according to one commentator, beyond the borderlands remains a distant, hostile, foreign, exotic state.[10] Although the borderlands might be considered from a northern perspective to be part of a bulwark to fence out the rest of the island, good fences also make good neighbours and 'mending the fences', which might be a metaphor for current British and Irish agreements on the border, may eventually lead to more convergence than contestation in the borderlands.

In the second place, there is the local view, where the border as a reality was subsumed into everyday life. This involved getting on with it and getting around it, living with it and, indeed, living off it. Harkness may be right here in referring to the porosity of the border. It was more real from a distance, from the centres. Historically, the state's continuous institutional border presence in daily life was the 'customs man' and, speaking from a southern vantage point, he was absorbed into the community. A schoolmaster's diary of the 1930s has customs men from exotic Gaeltacht areas in the west of Ireland lodging in local farmhouses, while he practised his Irish on them and bought northern butter and bread carried over the border fields by the schoolchildren – or, as Ó Faolain noted in 1940, when the border 'ceased to function' after six o clock.

Getting over this local obstacle was a normal state of affairs.

> You go over to the Gardaí who are guarding the border... and you ask them to find you a man who will take you as a passenger... [11]

Indeed the folklore of smuggling shows how much it was a part of 'normality', not just for the big profiteers, but for ordinary local people who found ways around it - like the man who used come to our house after dark with a box of butter on the carrier, or my mother's 'innocent' hiding of butter as she passed through the border. Nobody was really innocent in the borderlands. It turned us all into petty criminals. At eleven years of age, I 'imported' a bike load of squibs and rockets from Keady, walking with burning ears past the customs hut. One could talk also about the 'geographical moralities' of the borderlands, when the Roman Catholic diocese of Clogher which, straddling counties Monaghan and Fermanagh, remains a real geographical expression of the borderlands, banned Saturday night dancing while Armagh diocese did not. One could escape this 'reserved sin' by going over the Monaghan-Armagh border.

The stories about smuggling escapades in the borderlands, many of which were recorded in the Irish Folklore Commission's collections from the 1930s onwards, played a big role in local life by cutting the border down to size, representing local victories over its interference in everyday life and movement. In the 1940s, as well as cattle and pigs, eggs, flour and sugar were smuggled northwards. Flour bags filled with sugar were used as dummy pillows in the Clones area in 1940. During the Economic War there were advertisements in the Monaghan newspaper the *Northern Standard* for 'swimming cows'. Dozens of Northern purchasers were arrested in Monaghan for buying 'parcels' to take over the border in September 1941.

My father and others with family working and living in Belfast, frequently cycled back south over the border wearing several jumpers, trousers, or stockings purchased in the city. Years later an acquaintance from east Belfast told me that in the 1950s his mother and himself regularly travelled by train to shop in Clerys in Dublin, crossing back north overdressed in similar fashion. Inhabitants of the Glaslough borderlands would shop in the 1920s in Armagh and throw out their parcels along the railway line for collection by family members. In west Fermanagh, 'fishermen' from north and south used to row out on Lough Melvin and land on islands in the lake to exchange jewellery, watches, cigarettes, safety blades, perfume and whiskey.[12]

Songs and verses about such activities marked the ultimate celebration of such local triumphs, joining a rich vein of ballad tradition. The 'Border Bullock' commemorated a triumph over the customs men during the Economic War, part of a living tradition which was continued in the more recent song 'The Transit Van'.

> All you Customs Officials to your duty attend
> Not a six county man saw this bullock being penned,
> He came the same way as did thousands before
> That have all landed safely on England's fair shore.[13]

Although there was a modicum of unity in diversity in the borderlands, with a social cohesion that was inconveniently fractured, like similar areas everywhere they were contested spaces whose landscapes were marked by symbol to imprint their meanings on public consciousness. Growing up near the border, it marked the beginnings northwards of good roads and red telephone boxes.

One English visitor many years ago expressed the reality and intentionality of the symbolism, which struck visitors more forcibly than locals.

> I realised as I went through towns and villages in Ulster that perhaps the boundary was not so nebulous as I had thought it. For I seemed to be in England again. There were war memorials quite as bad as those at home. I saw a Union Jack flying on a railway station. The pillar-boxes were red. The postmen were like English postmen. All trivial things, but after the Free State, which is trying to make itself as Irish as possible, they printed themselves on the mind with agreeable sharpness….. but the hills were, beyond question, the hills of Ireland.[14]

Earlier, another visitor noted the English table sauces, the posters seeking boys for the Royal Navy, the union jacks and the constabulary with holstered pistols as distinctive features in the landscape.[15]

In Ireland the borderlands also signal the beginnings and origins of sectarian landscapes, where the balance of power teeters between communities. The Orange Order, founded in 1795, was born in Armagh and continues as a sort of politico-cultural marker up to the present. Marching is a territorial act and borderlands, if anything, are about territory.

> Drums thunder early on the 12th of July. At the far end of the town by the cattle
> mart, marchers and musicians mill, assembling while people dressed to stand the
> rain and chilly winds begin to line the main streets. Up and down bands parade,
> banging a martial beat between the fronts of shops and homes. Against the
> steady cannonade, booming, pounding, the lambeg drums rattle a battle call.
> Onward slowly, the big drums move, borne by a pair of men in hard hats, coats
> off, sleeves rolled to hot work, swivelling together to whack a rackety tattoo,
> whipping around them a wild storm of sound…[16]

'The marching season' has had particular visceral significance in the
borderlands. It is a 'marking' season to claim and demarcate the landscape with
the symbols of identity on one side or the other.

The 15th of August, with its nationalist tint, is a weak response to the 12th of
July, but it summons up other symbols in nearby landscapes:

> At Belcoo, after Mass, the crowd flows happily around the peddlers of food and
> raffle tickets, streaming along the street where bands march, bumping along the
> field where Gaelic footballers run and thump, breaking, eddying around
> platforms on which young dancers, embroidered over with ornament from the
> Book of Kells, bob and leap sternly for prizes….. the hoopla stand, the military
> post, twangy country-and-western music, march tunes and endless Irish reels
> roll through the trees and out over the lake. By night, celebrants join the pubs
> around the fiddlers and walk easily back and forth past the customs post and the
> earnest young men selling pamphlets, crossing and recrossing the bridge
> connecting the public houses of Belcoo with those of Blacklion…, intending their
> drink-strengthened stroll as an eradication of the Border.[17]

This has been a recurring experience, especially for the past eighty years.
Bands and banners are carried through landscapes and townscapes,
commemorating and embedding events in the community memory for
transmission into the future. Early on, in 1924, during the discussions of the
Boundary Commission, Newry witnessed

> a big day – Black Day, it was called – under the Auspices of the Imperial Grand
> Black Chapter of the British Commonwealth. Fourteen special trains had come
> from Belfast alone. Other trains ran from Tynan, Killylea, Armagh, Keady,
> Markethill, Hillsborough, Dromore, Downpatrick, Portadown, Scarva, Lisburn
> and other points north bearing the Sir Knights and their friends, in all nearly
> thirty thousand, to this, the greatest celebration which had ever taken place in the
> border town. This great meeting had gathered at Newry to show that the North
> was prepared to fight for its territory to the bitter end. It was a day of threats,
> thunders, disparagements and denunciations….[18]

The past thirty years have seen republican marching in other parts of the
borderlands, commemorating other events. 'Martyr Memorial bands' have led
parades to new monuments which mark the borders like mirror images of the
war memorials in other places to the dead of two world wars. Colm Tóibín's
pilgrimage through the borderlands in the late 1980s is a sometimes tense and
wary wending through fragile sectarian landscapes and verbal taboos, a
landscape fractured and stamped with the loaded symbolism of words, accents,
names, music, flags, churches, schools, pubs, monuments, as well as a tangible

fear of bomb and bullet.

Monaghan town was always a northern town in the 'South'. Having a Diamond and other signifiers of an Ulster lineage, it was a meeting place and stage for both traditions: the 12th of July in the forties and fifties, and Corpus Christi celebrations. My memory of Corpus Christi is of a peculiar demonstration that was more like the 12th of July in its colour and symbolism than the 15th of August. Monaghan marked the northern borders of the Catholic state where, like Northern Ireland on the Twelfth, all businesses closed, and shops had 'altar displays' with statues and emblems in their windows and doors. There were processions of priests and schoolchildren, confraternity men, and boy scouts. The FCA[19] paraded and there were elaborate canopies and banners, hymns culminating in 'Faith of our Fathers', and numerous yellow papal flags, bunting, and Irish tricolours.

Diaries of the 1930s, 40s and 50s record regular trips to Belfast and across the border by train. There was a big Monaghan community in Belfast, a place associated with holidays, picture houses, plays, and billiards, as well as annual excursion trains to Dublin for All-Ireland final day. At the local level, the borderlands were quite porous especially from the southern side. For Cavan, and for Monaghan particularly, Belfast had been the commercial centre and capital of Ulster and over the generations had produced strong kinship-links across the border, with summer holidays bringing visiting relatives home to Monaghan from Belfast and Scotland. My father, on his youthful trips north to family, occasionally accompanied his aunt's RUC (ex RIC) officer husband on patrol in Lurgan or Lack. There was less linkage southwards by Protestants. Indeed the years after the 1920s saw much Protestant movement to the northern borderlands, reflected in significant local population decline among the Protestant population in 'Ulster (part of)'.

Brian Graham and others have spoken of the negative, defensive identity of Ulster Protestants – defined in opposition to the otherness of what was perceived as a threatening Gaelic, Catholic south, which was particularly displayed in the borderlands.[20] John Hewitt, the northern poet who agonised over Protestant identity, was especially interested in landscape and belonging to place as a guide to identity, but in the end it seems his metaphor was one of occupying a 'faulted ledge' with the border landscape the fracture and edge of his world.[21]

Alice Milligan's 'When I was a little girl', written in the late nineteenth century, probably articulates fearful folk memories of Protestants in this vulnerable borderland, which were to loom again in the 1970s and 80s.

To hear of a night in March

And loyal folk waiting,

To see a great army of men

Come devastating.

An army of papists grim,

With a green flag o'er them,

Redcoats and black police

Flying before them.

But God (who our nurse declared

Guards British dominions)

Sent down a deep fall of snow

And scattered the Fenians.[22]

Writers from the borderlands are good witnesses to the centrality of land, its ownership and dispossession on these frontiers. Being displaced in the borderlands was the experience of many of the lower-level Gaelic inhabitants who became tenants on the new estates in the seventeenth and eighteenth centuries. As new settlers filtered in, the native population was displaced to the margins.[23] William Carleton described his familiar Aghintain landscape with the (un)certainties of folk memory in the pre-famine period:

> The father paused to take breath and supported by his spade, looked down upon the sheltered inland which, inhabited chiefly by Protestants and Presyterians, lay rich and warm-looking under him… the Catholics generally inhabit the mountainous part of the country, to which they had been driven at the point of the bayonet; the Protestants and Presbyterians on the other hand, occupy the richer and more fertile tracts of land…[24]

Holding on at the edge has been the more recent experience of many Protestant communities. 'Keeping the name on the land', a shared cultural phenomenon throughout Ireland, had a great significance for Protestant farming borderland communities in the twentieth century. The border from the 1920s acted as a sieve, with an ethnic sorting of people and townlands to the north and south. Eugene McCabe, a Monaghan writer living on the border, provides an astute perspective on this imperative of ownership in such contested landscapes:

> For Canon Leo McManus the best part of his ministry was travelling on horseback the by-roads, farms, villages and townlands of Upper Fermanagh. On the walls of his dining room in the parish house at Dromcoo he had land commission maps pencil-marked, and could tell at a glance the name, status and religion of the owner. He kept a separate register for emigrants, corresponding with those who had prospered and tried to persuade them to buy back, where possible, what he called in his circular 'The escheated or stolen patrimony of our forbears'….. the county was evenly divided between Catholics and Protestants; time and determination, God willing, would alter that.[25]

Genealogy of the borderland region

Geography matters in explanations of the historical origins of the border landscapes. They are undoubtedly products of the operation of basic geographical realities like location, distance, spatial relationships, peripherality, accessibility, territorial boundaries, remoteness and one very important reality in the process of change – geographical inertia, especially in relation to the stability of boundaries and territories. One of the important facts of life for all of us is how slowly the lines in our landscapes change, whether we talk about a field, a farm, a street or aggregates of these in townlands, parishes and counties. Patrick Kavanagh's *Epic* is a classic rendition of the power of these forces for territorial, as well as cultural, continuity in local spaces. The endurance of territorial boundaries is a fundamental reality in the Ulster borderlands. 'Not an inch' is an apposite slogan.

The historical evolution of the borderlands has been to a great extent shaped by their environmental legacy in land and soil.   The landscapes throughout south Ulster, for instance, exhibit qualities of the 'west' and the 'east' in the island of Ireland as a whole. The 'good' land of the east and the 'bad' land of the west are to be found in landscapes embracing Louth on the one hand and west Tyrone and Fermanagh on the other, sharing economic and social characteristics and problems with the east midlands of Ireland and the western regions of Connacht respectively. These environmental and economic characteristics played a significant role in the process of colonisation and settlement of the borderlands, a historical experience which has helped to consolidate their distinctiveness from the rest of Ulster and from regions in the midlands.   In this southern periphery of Ulster, Protestant settler immigration from the seventeenth century was hesitant and less coherent than further north, resulting in local segregation, landscapes that are honeycombed with ethnic and cultural differences, which became the ultimate contested borderland after the establishment of the official political boundary. These landscapes therefore also exhibit characteristics of 'north' and 'south': like many borderlands, it is a region of confusions and paradoxes.

In looking at the genesis of this region, passing reference may be made to the early historic significance of the Gap of the North, to the mythical hero Cuchulainn, who is an icon, from these borderlands, both of Irish nationhood and of loyalist separatism. But in terms of the historical distinctiveness of these landscapes, the medieval and early modern experience of the borderlands is most relevant. Pre-modern Ireland, like most pre-modern states, was a land of internal boundaries, marking one local political entity off from another. And one of the more enduring borderlands was certainly located in what today is south Ulster. European spatial order evolved from tribal lands to chiefdoms, to feudal and modern state systems of order, with integration into progressively more hierarchically ordered systems. The medieval Gaelic world, like most of medieval Europe, was a place where genealogical and territorial marginalisation occurred. In other words, those peoples who were most distant in kinship terms from the powerful elites ended up being displaced to the geographical margins of lordship territories. In the medieval period, most European landscapes were characterised by 'marchlands', where the political control of one entity faded out as another faded in. Frequently separate buffer territories developed as *ad hoc* survival stratagems by local communities, which fossilised with the emergence of modern states:

instead of space being organised through society [ie the localised tribal/clan/sept], it was now a case of society being organised through space. [shires,counties and borders][26]

In the new centralised modern state, the territorial reality of borders becomes more stringently defined, and irredentism less tolerated.

In many ways, Ireland fits into this frame. Its medieval fragmentation of authority resulted in local borders and unstable landscapes on the fringes of lordships. Border landscapes were frontier zones, often vulnerable to attack and oppression by one side on the other. It was sometimes called *fásach*, reflecting its wasteland character, often heavily wooded in the sixteenth century and characterised by disorder and instability.[27] In state records, there were quite complex definitions of the marches; for example, the 'English' or 'Irish' march, the 'Land of Peace', the 'Land of War'.

Throughout the medieval period south Ulster was a buffer zone which produced a number of small distinctive lordships whose survival depended on their facility to negotiate between the English Pale to the south and the Gaelic centres of power in the north. The O'Rourkes and MacClanceys of west Breifne, the O'Reillys, Maguires, MacMahons and O'Hanlons, who occupied the lake-strewn, inaccessible hilly country of south Ulster, controlled Gaelic territorial lordships which emerged in these frontier lands. The existence of this distinctive border region is probably best commemorated in the diocesan geographies of Clogher and Kilmore. In the late sixteenth century, one English commentator astutely observed that O'Donnell considered Maguire and O'Rourke to be "two hedges to his countrie, which hedges being broken down, his own countrie was to lie open to reformation."[28] This is what happened with the Plantation of Ulster, which one could characterise as an attempt by the modern English state to incorporate all the recalcitrant and fragmented extremities of the Gaelic world into its authority.

Why did the borderlands persist as a distinctive entity and how did their landscapes reflect their experience? The south Ulster borderlands, which had formerly been on the northern edge of the medieval English Pale, in the seventeenth century found themselves on the southern edge of the new 'colonial pale' centred in east Ulster. Its environmental conditions of hills and poor land, at a distance from the centres of colonial power contributed to a new peripherality. Its remoteness, comparative poverty and topographical difficulty made it relatively unattractive to settlers. Though Cavan was included in the Ulster Plantation, Monaghan was not, and it proved difficult to get new settlers into Farney in south Monaghan in spite of offers of favourable leases. Cavan was even farther from the centres to the east, so the plantation was less successful in parts of south Ulster. The settlement experience of this region, therefore, continued to be different and distinctive, as was its cultural and economic experience. Later attempts to integrate and settle some districts, continuing into the eighteenth century, only served to distinguish the region's social and cultural topography even more. New settlements, new farms and new roads in south Armagh, Cooley and other areas, for instance, established by planter settlers or displaced Gaelic people consolidated these differences. Newtownhamilton, Castleblaney, Newbliss, Smithborough, Virginia, Scotshouse, and Cootehill are some of the placename markers of this phase of settlement on the borders.

Religious intermingling illustrates some of the character of the borderlands. Maps show progressively larger Protestant populations as one moves north from Louth (90% Catholic) into Armagh and Monaghan. South Armagh and south Monaghan showed less than 10% Protestant in the first census on religion in 1861, but by mid Monaghan and mid Armagh it was 30-50% Protestant.[29] The townland, which was the primary unit of settlement from the earliest plantation experiments, continued as the basic landholding entity throughout the eighteenth century, and became the template for ethnic difference at local level. Thus a legacy of 'Protestant' and 'Catholic' townlands honeycomb the borderlands, a fragmented landscape reality which was familiar enough in Europe after the Treaty of Versailles in June 1919, and which was thus optimistically addressed by the Boundary Commission in 1925. It was a hopelessly complex problem however, a landscape riddle posed by two determined contestants that was abandoned in favour of the *status quo*, which fossilised the border essentially along the old Gaelic boundaries that had been instated in the sixteenth century as county boundaries.

The historical and settlement expression of this borderland region resulted in a distinctive demographic history. Its poor marginal lands divided into large landed estates in the seventeenth century provided suitable social and economic conditions for the successful development of the domestic linen industry. Strategically located on the southern edge of the emerging industrial heartland of Ulster, its small farm landscape was ideally suited to growing flax and the spinning and weaving of yarn. This economic phase facilitated a rapidly increasing rural population up to the famine period, when some of the largest Irish population densities over extensive areas featured in south Ulster. This resulted in the hugely fragmented farmscapes in the borderlands – tiny farms and a matching intricate lattice of small fields, cultivated by a teeming rural population. However, with the later nineteenth century contraction of the linen industry to the mills and factories of east Ulster, the south Ulster borderlands embarked on a long period of depopulation and decline as off-farm economic opportunities dwindled away. Emigration from the mid nineteenth century, faciliated by proximity to Newry, Belfast and Derry, became the hallmark of the region. Emigration from these marginal landscapes, on the economic peripheries of two states, continued to the United States and Britain into the 1930s, 40s and 50s. Patrick Kavanagh, a poet of the borderlands, wrote a dark poem called 'The Great Hunger' in 1942 which is a fitting elegy for a devastated landscape of incomplete and depopulated households on the borderlands of Ulster in middle of the twentieth century.[30]

For the past decade or so the borderlands have become the target of special measures like those supported by the International Fund for Ireland, or of economic, social or tourism policies sponsored by both states or the European

Union to revive and restore their fortunes. Programmes have been instigated to encourage 'cross border' initiatives, to try to restore the 'natural' economic, commercial or social hinterlands of urban centres and communities which have been bisected for generations by the border. Ironically, many of these policies may serve to continue to embed the distinctiveness of these landscapes as a region on the southern frontier of Ulster, on the northern edge of the Republic.

References

1 Colm Toíbín, *Walking along the border* (London 1987), p31.

2 L O'Dowd, 'What is a region? The case of the Irish borderlands' in P Ó Drisceoil, (ed), *Culture in Ireland. Regions: identity and power* (Belfast 1993:96), p96.

3 David Harkness, *Ireland in the twentieth century: divided island* (London 1996), p115.

4 O'Dowd, op. cit. p97.

5 S Bruce, 'Unionists and the border', in M Anderson and B Eberhard (eds), *The Irish border: history, politics, culture* (Liverpool 1999), pp133-135.

6 See also G Martin, 'The origins of partition' in Anderson and Eberhard (eds), op. cit..

7 Sean Ó Faolain, *An Irish journey* (New York 1940), p235.

8 H Speakman, *Here's Ireland* (New York 1925), p231.

9 Seamus Heaney, *Preoccupations: selected prose 1968-78* (London 1983), p18.

10 Bruce, op. cit. pp134-135.

11 Toíbín, op. cit. p70.

12 Irish Folklore Commission collection, vol 1609:13 (University College Dublin).

13 IFC 1937, S946:169.

14 H V Morton, *In Search of Ireland* (London 1930), pp231-232.

15 Speakman, op. cit. p234.

16 Henry Glassie, *Passing the time. Folklore and history of an Ulster community* (Dublin 1982), p218.

17 Ibid. p165.

18 Speakman, op. cit. pp269-70.

19 Irish: 'Forsa Cosanta Aitíuil' - the local defence force and army reserve.

20 Brian Graham, *In search of Ireland - a cultural geography* (London 1997).

21 Frank Ormsby, (ed) *The collected poems of John Hewitt* (Belfast 1991), pp9-10.

22 Quoted in O Dudley Edwards, (1999), 'The shaping of border identities before partition' in Anderson and Eberhard, op. cit. p222.

23 Philip Robinson, *The plantation of Ulster. British settlement in an Irish landscape, 1600-1670* (Dublin 1984), p103.

24 William Carleton, 'The poor scholar' in *Traits and stories of the Irish peasantry* (London 1865), p257.

25 Eugene McCabe, *Death and nightingales* (London 1992), p19.

26 R Dodgshon, *The European past: social evolution and spatial order* (London1987), p137.

27 P J Duffy, D Edwards, and E Fitzpatrick (eds) *Gaelic Ireland c1250-1650: Land, lordship and settlement* (Dublin 2001).

28 H Wood, (ed) *The chronicle of Ireland 1584-1608*, by Sir James Perrott (Dublin 1933), p79.

29 P J Duffy, 'Geographical perspectives on the borderlands' in R Gillespie and H O'Sullivan, (eds) *The borderlands: essays on the history of the Ulster-Leinster border* (Belfast 1989), p16-17.

30 Patrick Kavanagh, *The complete poems of Patrick Kavanagh* (New York 1972).

The Black Pig's Dyke: a forgotten border

Aidan Walsh

Across the landscape of modern-day County Monaghan stretches a sinuous and substantial earthwork known to local people as 'The Black Pig's Dyke', 'The Worm Ditch' or the 'Black Pig's Race'.[1] It has long been the subject of speculation and scholar and layman have frequently discussed its purpose and age. Its folklore attributes it to legendary events set in a magical past.

In 1982 I directed an archaeological excavation on the Dyke to try and shed some light on these matters.[2] I published my excavation twice, firstly in *Emania* in 1987[3] and secondly, more fully in the 1991 *Clogher Record*.[4] I refer the reader to these publications for further detail, especially in regard to the archaeological excavation itself. I also recommend a visit to Monaghan County Museum where a scale model can be seen, showing the Dyke as it was when in use.

Nearly twenty years later, the results of the 1982 excavation still constitute the best archaeological evidence about the purpose, date, function and origin of this archaeological monument and feature in the standard archaeological textbooks used in our universities.[5]

The Black Pig's Dyke is a linear earthwork that winds its way across the land in much the same way as Hadrian's Wall, the Great Wall of China, or the late

The Black Pig's Dyke in Aghareagh West, showing the double bank and ditches. The land slopes from north to south, left to right of the picture.

fortified border between the two Germanys. It runs approximately east-west and, although often substantial, it is frequently denuded or incorporated into field fences and not always easy to see. Where best preserved it is usually double-banked and double-ditched. At Aghareagh West, near Scotshouse, County Monaghan, where the dig took place, the earthwork was 24 metres wide from north to south and survived to a maximum height of 1.5m and was originally probably twice that height. Excavation showed that the main ditch was originally also 2m deep. Taken together and allowing for the denuding of the bank itself, the north bank and ditch combine to form an obstacle which was originally at least 5m high. All in all, it was a substantial feature that stretched for miles. Its construction required considerable organisation and labour. Yet its real purpose is forgotten.

If you examine the 1910 Ordnance Survey maps you will see that three miles of the Dyke still stood then in County Monaghan and a further three miles are marked 'site of' by the surveyors, indicating its former course. Field walking in 1982 showed us that most of the three miles shown on the 1910 OS 6 inch edition still stand today. In Ireland generally, an attempt to establish the extent of the Dyke was made in the 1950s by Glaslough writer Sir Shane Leslie and an American academic, Brandon Barringer. They walked along linear earthworks from coast to coast between Bundoran, County Donegal, and Dundalk in County Louth and established that fifteen miles were still standing.[6]

Field walking in 1982 in Monaghan also showed that the Dyke is consistently constructed on the south facing slopes of the drumlins it traverses and that the smaller bank and ditch invariably lies downhill on the southern side of the hills.

In 1835 the great John O'Donovan wrote in the Ordnance Survey letters about the large scale of the Dyke saying:

> It runs almost from one extremity of the parish to the other in a south-easterly direction. As the people are plagued with it, striving to pay rent for it, they are labouring to level it with great industry and it is completely defaced in various fields, but up the sides of barren hills it still shows its double ditch and broad rampart in all its pristine perfection, defying on its way through the plantation and across the summits of unprofitable hills the pick axe of the covetous farmer for at least another century. It must have been a tremendous Ollpheist[7] that ran across the country when she formed so deep a track, but her coils so voluminous and vast, cannot have been more terrible than the tusks of the huge boar that rooted up the Valley of the Black Pig.

O'Donovan refers in this passage to the folk explanations for the Dyke, to which I will refer further below. But what actually is the Black Pig's Dyke?

William Francis De Vismes Kane, of Drumreask House near Monaghan town, was a scholar and member of the Royal Irish Academy. In the early twentieth century he wrote two speculative papers where he combined actual observation on the ground with folklore and placenames to conclude that Ireland had three cross-country earthworks, two in the midlands and the third in south Ulster.[8] We are looking at his Ulster line, the only one at all plausible today. This line connects the Danes Cast on the Armagh/Down border with the

Dorsey in south Armagh, a Dyke fragment at Lough Muckno in mid-Monaghan, and our stretch near Scotshouse in west Monaghan. He also extended his line further westwards to include some earthworks near Bundoran.

In his 1909 paper, Kane also quoted some nineteenth century accounts of accidental discoveries along the Dyke, as follows:

> In the townland of Lettercrossan, Patrick MacDonnell remembers that in emptying a fosse, on the Monaghan side (northern), of 5 or 6 feet depth of mud, there were found at regular intervals along the side, battens or balks of round timber resting against the original slopes as though they were stays. One end was pointed and charred, and driven into the ground. Also horizontal sleepers were found lying transversely across the bottom of about 2 to 2.5 feet in length, and roughly mortised at each end to the sloping side timbers.

This account assumes another meaning when the excavation yielded some secrets, as will be seen later. Lettercrossan is now spelled Lattacrossan and is the neighbouring townland to the excavation site.

So, what was the Black Pig's Dyke? O'Donovan believed it to be the ancient boundary of the south Ulster kingdom of Oriel. Interestingly, he mentioned a local County Monaghan tradition that the boundary formed a boundary between kings in ancient times. This is one of the very rare popular references to a practical function for the Dyke. With John O'Donovan we see the start of a trend to link the various scattered earthworks in south Ulster together to make one contemporary and continuous work. There was no evidence for that belief but Kane was not to be hindered by lack of evidence. His work is of great importance in drawing attention to the linear earthworks and to making the study of the Dyke a serious scholarly subject. Yet he speculated wildly and posited three earthworks in Ireland, each cross-country and each a boundary. Evidence on the ground was extremely thin, especially for his two southernmost lines, but he believed that the northern one was erected around 200AD to defend Ulster from attack.

Oliver Davies[9] believed that the monument formed the southern boundary of the kingdom of Ulster and was constructed in imitation of Roman frontier lines. The post-Roman date also accorded well with tradition about the alleged fifth century destruction of the capital of Ulster, Emain Macha (Navan Fort near Armagh City) and the collapse of the kingdom of Ulster. The linear earthworks were said to be connected to the Ulster wars and the epic stories of the Ulster Cycle. Until the 1982 excavation and another on the Dorsey linear earthwork in south Armagh, most archaeologists believed that the Dyke and similar sites were post-Roman in date, copied by the Irish and dating to the first centuries after Christ.

The excavation in 1982 was a short, four-week, undertaking. A well-preserved section was selected and a trench dug across and followed down to the original ground surface. Disappointingly, there were no discoveries of artefacts and little evidence of any kind. Because the nineteenth century

The larger north bank, fully excavated down to original ground surface.

accounts described substantial wooden remains from the adjacent fields in the neighbouring townland, similar remains were expected at Agareagh west. We were to be disappointed in this also.

The interesting discovery came in the third week when the top of a deep backfilled trench was found just a metre back from the edge of the northern ditch. This transpired to be a slot of almost 1m depth and tapering from a half metre-wide mouth to a 30cm-wide base. It was full to overflowing with a mixture of oak charcoal, burned clay and blackened stones. Indeed, so intense had been the fire that the walls of the trench were baked red to a depth of 7cms. In three other places nearby, the slot was also uncovered, in addition to an accidental discovery of a further exposure one mile away to the west in the townland of Aghnaskew. The charcoal was sampled for Carbon 14 dating, a laboratory technique which can establish the approximate date of organic remains.

It is quite clear that a deep slot had been dug, into which was set a substantial palisade or fence of oaken timber, probably tree trunks. This fence may have been up to 5m high and formed a third line in parallel to the main double banks and ditches themselves. The palisade was later deliberately burned to the ground. The nineteenth accounts of the finding of partly burned timbers next door in Lattacrossan almost certainly represent a survival of better-preserved intact and unburnt remains of the palisade.

With the return of the charcoal from Carbon 14 laboratories in Belfast and the Netherlands, the destruction was dated to a wide bracket of 500-25 BC.

The palisade trench; fully excavated this sizeable trench was big enough to accommodate an archaeologist.

Charcoal can not provide close dates, unlike wood which can be dated frequently to the year and even the season of its felling.

Taken together, the excavation yielded some remarkable results. Firstly, the Black Pig's Dyke is a prehistoric construction, not a Christian era monument. Secondly it was built before the Roman armies entered Britain. Thirdly it was in all likelihood a native Irish concept and not copied from Roman military prototypes. Fourthly, the excavation showed it to be a serious defensive work, facing south to counter a threat from that direction. Fifthly, it was a three-line defence, not simply a double bank and ditch. In addition, it was systematically destroyed, probably during wartime. The Dyke was also shown to be more than a mere anti-cattle rustling barrier, a common practice in ancient Ireland. It was too big and strong and too extensive to be that. It was clearly a tribal boundary and defence.

The palisade stood for at least one mile in this area of County Monaghan, the accidental Aghnaskew exposure vouching for that. It may well have paralleled the Dyke for the six well-attested miles in the county. Such a defence took considerable organisation and resources to erect. Bear in mind also that the palisade was made of oak, whereas alder and hazel dominated the tree pollen found during the dig. In other words the oak was not growing locally and had to be imported into the district.

As to date, the evidence from the dig places the destruction of the Dyke within a very broad time span but the information from the Dorsey excavation

General view during excavation, looking south towards the larger north bank. The smaller south bank is hidden from view; in the foreground the palisade trench is beginning to appear.

by Chris Lynn[10] also needs to be taken into account. There, he found the remains of a substantial oak palisade, which was also deliberately destroyed around 100 BC. We must also look at the date of the destruction of Navan, which archaeology now also places around 100 BC.[11] These precise dates were produced through dendro-chronology (tree ring dating). In the absence of wood at Aghareagh West our dating cannot be so precise but they are certainly not incompatible with the other dates. Further excavation leading to the recovery of intact timbers would permit a close dating.

I have speculated in the past about the context for the destruction of the Black Pig's Dyke. We are dealing with a substantial frontier composed of earthwork and palisade, erected as tribal boundary and defence, destroyed perhaps in a war, which extended across the land, starting at the borders of a kingdom and culminating with the destruction of its capital, Emain Macha. It is a fascinating picture, but one that is yet very unclear and unproven.

What then of the popular or folk memory of the Dyke. As places fall into disuse and new generations replace the previous, so too knowledge about function and origin is lost and distorted. In time, the purpose of abandoned monuments is often completely forgotten and replaced with popular beliefs that seek to explain their existence. Is this what happened to the Black Pig's Dyke? In the nineteenth century, John O'Donovan recorded a local tradition that the Dyke was a defence and boundary but the overwhelming evidence from the folk record is otherwise.

Fionnuala Williams[12] has chronicled the extensive folklore surrounding the Dyke. Some folk stories do indeed talk of the earthworks being built by the Danes or as forming boundaries in ancient times. But in recounting beliefs about the origin of the Dyke she demonstrates that the most common and widespread belief about the origin of linear earthworks is the one concerning the Black Pig. She cites fifty examples of this legend that were collected by folklorists over many decades, the earliest record being O'Donovan's 1835 example. The Department of Irish Folklore at University College Dublin collected her most recent example in 1975 in County Cavan. Examples are found in at least sixteen counties in all the provinces, although the largest numbers were recorded in Meath and Cavan. The legend usually opens with a reference to the dyke or 'race' of the black pig and then tells of a schoolmaster who could work magic. At first no one was aware of this but once it was discovered, he was overcome, usually by magic and forced to flee in the form of the pig. The course of his flight is marked by the Dyke, which he gouged out as he fled.

A quarter of the recorded folktales about the pig refer to the Dyke by name, even though the stories are not immediately local. The monument itself clearly lived on by name in folk memory but its true purpose was almost entirely forgotten. The Black Pig's Dyke is a forgotten border which still in places parallels the county boundary between Monaghan and Cavan, set back a field or two from the present line. The fact that its boundary function was not remembered points up the gulf that can often exist between popular memory and reality.

Notes and references

1 The best-preserved stretch of the Dyke can be seen and visited in the townland of Aghareagh West, near Scotshouse, County Monaghan. National Grid H5117; OS 6" sheet 21. 14cms from E, 6cms from W.

2 Aidan Walsh was Curator of Monaghan County Museum from 1974 - 1989 and undertook the dig in that capacity, funded by the Royal Irish Academy/National Committee for Archaeology.

3 *Emania, Bulletin of the Navan Research Group*, Vol.3 (1967) pp5-11.

4 *Clogher Record, Journal of the Clogher Historical Society*, Vol XIV, No I, 1991.

5 John Waddell, *The Prehistoric Archaeology of Ireland* (Galway 1998).

6 Brandon Barringer. 'On the Track of the Black Pig', *University Museum Bulletin*, vol.19, No.1, March 1955, (University of Pennsylvania).

7 Irish for huge serpent or worm.

8 W F De Vismes Kane, 'The Black Pig's Dyke: the Ancient Boundary Fortifications of Uladh', *Proceedings of the Royal Irish Academy*, 27C (1909) No.14, and Kane, 'Additional Researches on the Black Pig's Dyke', PRIA 33C (1917) No.19.

9 Oliver Davies, 'Excavations on the Dorsey and the Black Pig's Dyke', *Ulster Journal of Archaeology*, Vol 3 (1940), pp31-37.

10 C J Lynn, 'The Dorsey and other Linear Earthworks' in B G Scott (ed) *Studies on Early Ireland - Essays in honour of M V Duignan*. (Belfast 1982).

11 M G L Baillie, 'The Centre Post from Navan Fort', *Emania*, Vol 1 (1986) pp 20-21.

12 Fionnuala Williams. 'The Black Pig's Dyke and Linear Earthworks', *Emania,* 3, (1987) pp12-19.

Exhibiting religion

Linda McKenna

One of the concerns many commentators expressed during the course of preparations for marking the year 2000 was that there was not enough emphasis on the Christian aspect of the Millennium. Some felt that the birth of Jesus Christ was being forgotten in a celebration packed with fireworks and parties. Down County Museum's Millennium programme aimed to redress that imbalance. We wanted to draw people into an examination of challenging and difficult issues while retaining an accessible style and story.

In early 1999 we began planning the museum's programme of events for the Millennium year. We decided that the centrepiece would be an exhibition dealing with the history of Christianity in County Down from the coming of St Patrick to the present day. Supporting the exhibition was to be a comprehensive programme of events including talks, lectures and debates, performing arts events, music, children's and family events, and a film festival.

The programme was designed to encourage people to explore their history and cultural heritage in thought provoking but lively ways, and to contextualise the huge story of our Christian heritage within the framework of County Down. We previously had great success in 1998 with our 'When Down was Up' commemoration of the 1798 Rising, when we took one central theme as the inspiration for a year-long programme and so gave strong focus to our interpretative efforts. The success of this model encouraged us to try to develop it in 2000 with another theme which undoubtedly has continuing relevance to our society.

Before going into the detail of what our exhibition on Christianity in County Down entailed, it is important to emphasise some of the other elements which made up our events programme.

We had a lecture series in the museum, 'Examining the past with the future in mind', which was financially assisted by the Northern Ireland Millennium Festival Fund. A range of speakers spoke on a variety of topics in which religion was an element, including perceptions of Irishness, parading in Northern Ireland, education in Northern Ireland, the history of the RUC, and the Act of Union in County Down.

We ran a film festival featuring films with a faith, hope, or charity theme, ranging from *A Man for All Seasons* to *Schindler's List*, in conjunction with the Upstairs Film Theatre in Downpatrick. We organised guided bus tours around sites of religious significance in the county, and the work done to prepare these, and previous tours based on 1798 Rising sites, now forms part of the repertoire we can offer to groups who wish to buy services from the museum.

Our community play, *Prisoners, Pikes and Preachers* was a collaboration with a series of local schools and the 'History Through Drama' theatre in education group. The idea was to raise awareness of the importance of the town of Downpatrick's from its heyday as one of the foremost ecclesiastical centres in Ireland to its role as the judicial and administrative capital of the county. We used two performance spaces for the play, the museum courtyards (in what was the old county gaol) and the adjacent Down Cathedral, and the audience followed the actors from one place to the other. This was not a costumed, representational drama but more of a physical theatre piece focusing on the presentation of historical events through movement, voice, music and use of choruses. The project was grant aided by the MGM Millennium Festival fund and the local authority's Community Relations section.

Our exhibition was called 'Spreading the Word'. It told the story of spreading the Christian message through the experiences of some personalities connected with County Down, from the fifth to the twentieth centuries.

During planning meetings for the exhibition we considered various ways of recounting the history of Christianity in County Down. Initially, being a museum we, of course, thought about a 'letting the objects speak for themselves' mode of exhibition. The problem about this approach was that we didn't have a lot of objects and those that we did have illustrated what you might call material church history rather than conveying the conviction of peoples' religious beliefs and experiences. We did not want simply displays of statues, church fabric, religious vestments and 'uniforms', with banners, books and medals. This would have been an exhibition very similar to the 'Symbols' exhibition produced comparatively recently as an exercise to help community relations in Northern Ireland. This was important in its own right but not necessarily about 'spreading the word' or addressing the problematical (for a museum) questions of non-material motivation and conviction.

We then thought about a denominational approach, recounting the history of each of the main denominations in County Down and displaying objects and stories relating to each of these. The merits of this approach would probably have been be an increased awareness of community relations issues and better understanding of similarities and differences which are crucially important for us today. However we thought that such an exhibition might be overtly didactic for the occasion and might risk being seen as 'worthy but dull'.

In the end we decided to try to combine all of our aims. As a museum, objects had to be central. As a museum with a strong community relations focus for our work we wanted to show the actuality of our history and its echoes today; and as a community museum with a strong educational and public service ethos we wanted to make the story accessible. After much discussion we decided to look at a series of actual evangelists, in the broadest possible sense, with County Down connections who had brought Christ's message to a variety of people in a variety of ways. We did this by creating a series of life-size dioramas representing these people, as follows:

St Patrick: We all think we know quite a lot about St Patrick, although he is probably one of the most unknowable of the great figures of Irish history. Nevertheless we do know more than many people think, and since the museum was first established in the 1980s, on the Hill of Down near Patrick's traditional burial place, it has presented the generally accepted evidence about Patrick without recourse to myth. We think that Patrick probably grew up in a Romanised settlement near Hadrian's Wall in what is now northern England; that as a youth he was captured by Irish raiders and sold into slavery; that his faith sustained him in times of hardship and that following his escape from slavery he returned to Ireland as a missionary bishop. He probably landed in County Down in the first half of the fifth century and established his first church at Saul. We have two written documents which scholars believe to derive from him and which show him to have been a strong evangelical with extensive biblical knowledge. He was so successful in the conversion of notable chiefs and their followers, and his legend became so strong that he became our patron saint. He is probably buried in or around Downpatrick.

St Malachy: St Malachy was born in Armagh around 1094. He was ordained as a priest at the age of just twenty-five. At this time the Celtic church had developed in its own way and become independent of Rome. It was dominated by monasteries ruled by abbots. However the papacy wanted the Irish church to conform to the Roman organization, a wish Malachy embraced. He too wanted to Romanise and reform the Irish church. Despite strong resistance he was successful.

The monks of Greyabbey: Greyabbey was a Cistercian monastery, founded in 1193, by John de Courcy's wife, Affreca. It was one of the richest in County Down. The Reformation reached Ireland in 1536. One of the most profound effects of the Reformation was the dissolution of the monasteries like Greyabbey.

Robert Jackson and his family were a representation of the Scottish Presbyterian settlers who came to north Down in the seventeenth century. Presbyterian church government is based on individual congregations and is different from the hierarchical system of both the Anglican and Roman Catholic churches. Initially this was tolerated by the Anglican bishops. However, in the tense conditions of the 1630s, leading to the English Civil War, such independence frightened rulers. In 1639 Charles I's Irish Deputy, Thomas Wentworth, made all Scots settlers in Ulster, over sixteen years old, swear publicly to obey royal commands. Magistrates forced families to take it on their knees and our diorama showed such a scene of forced adherence to what became known as the 'Black Oath'. Wentworth swore to prosecute all who refused, and drive them from Ireland 'root and branch'. Many County Down settlers fled back to Scotland.

Bishop Jeremy Taylor was a powerful Anglican theological writer who opposed Puritan ideas prevalent during the 'reign' of Oliver Cromwell. As a chaplain to Charles I he was loyal to the crown and was accused of stirring up Royalist opposition to Cromwell. In 1654, under the Puritan Commonwealth,

Diorama: the Jackson family.

he was gaoled for preaching in London in defence of the Book of Common Prayer. He came to Ireland in 1658 to avoid more imprisonment. On the restoration of the monarchy in 1660, Taylor went to Dublin to re-establish Anglicanism at Trinity College. In 1661 he was made Bishop of Down, Connor and Dromore. Our diorama showed him in front of the foundations of Dromore Cathedral which he rebuilt in that year. Taylor took a hard line with Presbyterian ministers. Ironically, for a man who wrote a pamphlet called *The Liberty of Prophesying*, he barred thirty-seven Presbyterian ministers from occupying Anglican parishes.

Margaret Davidson: Born in Killinchy on the shores of Strangford Lough, she was inspired by the preaching of John Wesley, and became one of the itinerant lay preachers characteristic of Methodism. Despite her poverty and blindness, she supported herself by spinning and travelled the County Down countryside, alone, to preach. John Wesley first came to Ireland in 1747. He visited County Down many times in the next forty years, spreading the word. He preached in the Grove, below Down Cathedral, standing on a pedestal on which there had once been a statue of Saint Patrick.

Diorama: Margaret Davidson, and exhibition of objects associated with Christian observance.

Patrick Dorrian was born in Downpatrick in 1814. His early education was at the school of the liberal Presbyterian minister of the town, the Reverend James Neilson. After attending Maynooth, Dorrian became a curate in Belfast. He was parish priest of Loughinisland during the Great Famine. In 1865 he became Bishop of Down and Connor. He faced the problems in Belfast of a growing Roman Catholic population and sectarian rivalries. Riots were frequent. Dorrian responded by providing more churches, priests and schools, and supporting charity work and temperance crusades. He supported Parnell's Home Rule movement but opposed fenianism and violence. Our diorama showed him presiding over the building of the large Catholic church in Downpatrick and the convent and schools brought to the town by the Sisters of Mercy.

Sidney Elisabeth Croskery provided an example of a twentieth century missionary. Irish missionaries of all denominations are famous for their work abroad. Sidney Croskery, whose family were originally from County Down, was born in 1901. She went to school in Belfast and then trained as a doctor in Edinburgh. A dedicated pacifist, she became a Quaker as war loomed in the 1930s. At school she wanted to be a medical missionary. Most Christian denominations have missionary orders and societies, following the footsteps of the early disciples. In 1939, Sidney joined the Church of Scotland Mission in the Yemen. Here, she provided pioneering medical treatment, especially for women, and our diorama showed her as the first western doctor to be allowed admission to the harem. In terrible conditions and with severe shortage of medicine, she treated typhoid, tuberculosis and many eye diseases. In 1945 she ran the Child Welfare Clinic in Aden. She travelled extensively to inoculate children against malaria, sometimes even helping spray insecticide on mosquito swamps.

C S Lewis: The first part of the twentieth century was a time of crisis for many Christians. New philosophies, scientific discoveries and the horrors of the Great War made religion difficult to believe in. After military service in the war, Lewis went to Oxford where, after graduating, he became an academic and a writer. He became a convinced Christian and used his literary skills to promote religion. Books like *Mere Christianity* (1952) became best sellers and the 'Narnia' series of books continue to present a Christian allegory to children. Broadcasts like *Christian Behaviour* (1943) found many willing ears during the bleak wartime years. They made complex religious questions relevant to any listener. After Churchill, his was the best-known radio voice. He once said that his idea of heaven would be to have the spires of Oxford among the hills of Down.

Diorama: C S Lewis.

Accompanying these displays of individuals and their stories was a series of selected artefacts from the museum's collection. These included a bible quilt, early Christian grave slabs, paintings of the Nativity, items commemorating St Patrick and St Patrick's Day, bibles, hymn books and prayer books. A participative exhibit asked visitors what they thought about issues ranging from women priests to the future of Christianity itself. The juxtaposition of a traditional display of religious artefacts with the representation of the missionary 'impulse' in the diorama displays encouraged visitors to the exhibition to think about Christianity in more depth and to engage with some of the thoughts and theories of individuals from all the major Christian denominations. It was therefore possible for visitors to encounter differences of religious opinion and to learn more about the history of religion in Northern Ireland in a safe environment and in an unforced way.

The museum's accompanying programme of events enabled further examination and participation by people who wanted to explore issues in more detail. Further information and research on the theme was given permanent form in the museum's Yearbook for 2000. This was entirely dedicated to articles on different aspects of Christianity in County Down, paying particular attention to objects in the museum collection and to the challenges which exist for museums in representing aspects of culture which are not material but, none the less, real.[1]

By these various means we hope to have given some depth to our presentation of objects and ideas to people of all ages. At the same time we intended to provide both education and enjoyment for people who simply visited the museum for an informal day out.

Note

1 Brian S Turner (ed), *Down Survey 2000: The Yearbook of County Down Museum* (Downpatrick 2000).

Scottish borderers on an Irish frontier: the transformation of Lancie Armstrang

Brian S Turner

We thought that 'The Debateable Land' was a good title for our conference at this time, in this place, when so many borders, boundaries, and interfaces in our land are being debated. As you know, the term comes from Britain. It was used in the sixteenth century for a small area, just north of Carlisle, which was called the Debateable Land because it was disputed between England and Scotland.

As well as providing a title for our conference the Debateable Land has many other resonances for us in south Ulster. I have called one of them 'Lancie Armstrang'.

We all know that history is about today rather than yesterday. It is a means of discovering, or perhaps simply rationalising, where we are now. And so we tend to find the history we are looking for. That being so, it seems wise to look for as many different histories as we can.

My story has a very specific focus, but it contains an appeal of general relevance to us all today. It arises from my interest in family names. Names can be used, not just for individual genealogical purposes, but as indicators of the various strands which have wound together to make our community. That factor has led to considerable abuse and misinformation, and more light needs to be cast.

The surnames of County Fermanagh, for example, have a unique characteristic in Ulster. Unusually the name of the dominant pre-Plantation family, Maguire, is the commonest surname in the present day. Its offshoots, especially the McManuses and McCaffreys, are also very numerous. But in Fermanagh a small number of surnames of British origin have also proliferated strongly and widely, to such an extent that, uniquely in the Plantation counties, three of these names, Johnston, Armstrong, and Elliott, are among the five most numerous in the county.[1] That brings me back to 'Lancie Armstrang', and to 1603.

In that year society on the Anglo-Scottish border was fundamentally changed when James VI of Scotland became also James I of England. This was particularly so at the western end of the marches between Carlisle and Dumfries and especially in the Debateable Land and the valley of Liddesdale just north of the border. There a particular society had grown out of the circumstances of a remote borderland between two often unfriendly states. It was dominated by large independent family groups and characterised by fierce independence, lawlessness, tower houses, and kinship loyalty. Among its residents were 'Fire the Braes' Elliott, Nebless Clemmie Crozier, Willie Kang Irvine, Fingerless Will Nixon, and such men as Kinmont Willie Armstrong and another William Armstrong known as 'Ill Will'. Struggling officialdom described the family of Lancie Armstrong of Whithaugh as a 'bloodie and theevish clan'.

But in 1611, only eight years after King James moved south to London from Edinburgh a note appeared, among many others, in a small corner of the administrative records of the new state of affairs. 'Thom, Jok and Lancie Armstrangis…sall pass furth of the kingdomes of Scotland and England, and sall not returne…'[2]

That was at the end of almost a decade of terror on the Anglo-Scottish border. Some might say that it was the end of several centuries of terror as the new state sought to bring to an end the life of the border families by death, persecution and banishment. Those who had been a pain in the extremities of England and Scotland were now caught in the 'middle shires' of the new United Kingdom. They might, indeed, be described as the first victims of that Union.

They were identified and characterised by their surnames, just like the clans of Ireland and Highland Scotland. In the very first year of James' reign from London thirty two Armstrongs, Elliotts,

The Milnholm Cross, in the heart of Liddesdale, was traditionally erected about 1320 in memory of Alexander Armstrong, Laird of Mangerton, after his murder in Hermitage Castle.

Johnstons, Beatties and other borderers were hanged, fifteen were caught and expelled from the country and 140 were outlawed. The process went on remorselessly for years. The lands of the Grahams were confiscated and in 1605 150 of them were listed for transportation to the Low Countries, and the following year 124 were deported to Roscommon. None of this worked. The borderers would not stay where they were put.[3] And the list of outlaws marked for death grew into the hundreds, and their roll-call echoes across the years, and resounds around and along the Ulster border counties today. Armstrong, Johnston, Elliott, Nixon, Noble, Bell, Graham, Maxwell, Hall, Foster, Beattie, Little, Crozier, Irvine, Storey, Rutledge, Trimble.

My point is not to repeat a story you already know. I just draw attention to the fact that, at the same time as the Armstrongs and their neighbours were being killed or driven from their homes in Britain as part of government policy, that same government was pursuing a policy of Plantation in Ulster, for which it needed settlers. And the names of the earliest settlers on the south western fringes of the Plantation, farthest from Scotland, are dominated

At Longtown, Cumbria, at the foot of Liddesdale and Eskdale.

At Florencecourt, County Fermanagh.

by the Armstrongs, including at least two Lancie Armstrongs, Elliotts, Johnstons, Nixons and the rest.[4]

And that brings us back to the very particular features of the modern surnames of County Fermanagh. Its contemporary surname distribution draws our attention to the fact that Fermanagh has a particular relationship to an episode in British history which is quite unlike any other county.[5] We might suggest that exploring this factor could be helpful in understanding its evolution to the present day.[6]

Of the many points which can be drawn from this observation I will restrict myself to these:

Gaelic Ireland has a proud tradition of interest in genealogy and family history. This tradition of Catholic and aristocratic Ireland lamented the disruption caused by conquest and settlement in the seventeenth century. It was natural for poets and scholars to express bitter feelings of political and cultural defeat, and we can learn much from appreciating the feelings of that time. What is not defensible is that, even in our own day, some local histories can still speak of Irish people who bear surnames formed in Britain as if they were aliens in their own land, and collude accordingly.[7]

Four hundred years after the Plantation of Ulster we should be able to view the scene through a wider lens, and recognise the picture as it has developed.

Maguire and Johnston, both natives and neighbours, Main Street, Blacklion, County Cavan.

One of the things we can see is that, from their perspective, many of the settlers in early Plantation Fermanagh may also have felt themselves to be victims of political and cultural defeat, and of confiscation, displacement and death. In appreciating that possibility, local historians are in a good position to interrogate and to complicate such dangerously simplistic notions as 'The native Irish', 'The two traditions', or 'The Ulster Scots'.

We could do more to appreciate that the settlers in seventeenth century Ulster did not spring fully formed into existence simply to disrupt Irish society, but had long, and sometimes painful, previous histories of their own. But it is important also to carry on this logic and to be quite clear that the Armstrongs and Elliotts of today are not the Anglo-Scottish borderers of yesterday. Centuries of intermarriage and a myriad of relationships has made them a product of this land.

Take religion, for example. There are Armstrongs and Elliotts, and Maguires for that matter, inside and outside all the churches of Fermanagh. But this is not the land of Scots Presbyterians which we can see in other parts of Ulster. The Protestantism which is associated with many of the descendants of the borderers can be argued to be a product not of Britain, but of Ireland. The religious reputation of the borderers in Britain was summed up in the often repeated story of the person who inquired if there were any Christians in Liddesdale, only to be told that there were not, only Armstrongs and Elliotts.

But circumstances in Ireland associated the borderers with Anglican landowners, and later the first Methodist enthusiasts in Fermanagh included Armstrongs, Grahams, Johnstons, Beatties, Nixons and the rest.[8] And the comparatively smaller percentage of Presbyterians and larger percentage of Methodists is another thing which marks out Fermanagh among the Ulster counties.

So Lancie Armstrang's relatives and descendants are far removed from the wild days of murder and mayhem on England's north-west frontier. And yet, perhaps they still face the trials and challenges of frontiers, whether it be as farmers or shopkeepers in rural Ulster, or standing unaware at Enniskillen's Cenotaph, or indeed moving across the American continent or setting foot on the moon.[9]

They are part of the wonderful variety in our history and can help us to do our duty in complicating simplicity and confounding stereotypes.

And yet, having cautioned against stereotypes, perhaps we might still be allowed to encourage interest in the long, developing, heritage which, in one of its phases, led a sixteenth century Scottish writer to begin his poem with the lines,

On the border was the Armstrangs, able men;
Somewhat unruly, and very ill to tame.[10]

Notes and references

1 Brian S Turner, *An alphabetical list of the family names of County Fermanagh* (Belfast 1974).
2 These references to the Anglo-Scottish border country and some of its personalities are from George MacDonald Fraser, *The Steel Bonnets* (London 1974).
3 Ibid.
4 See, for example, 'County Fermanagh' in Seamus Pender (ed), *A Census of ireland, circa 1659* (Dublin 1939); and Peadar Livingstone, *The Fermanagh Story* (Enniskillen 1969), pp 446-466.
5. Many of these surnames had, and have, representatives on both sides of the Anglo-Scottish border. They are widespread in northern Ireland, and some have come at different periods. It is their particular concentration in Fermanagh, from the earliest years of seventeenth century settlement, which marks out this county.
6 Brian S Turner, 'An observation on settler names in Fermanagh' in *Clogher Record*, vol. viii, no.3, (1974), pp-285-289.
7 For example, with great fraternal respect one might ask what precisely was the significance and purpose of publishing the following quotation from the private letter of a distinguished Irish historian, on the occasion of his death, in 1974 when community tension and awful violence was very high in the area mentioned, and what message could Protestant and Catholic people in east Tyrone be expected to take from it?: 'I was charmed with everything, with the Irish and Catholic spirit everywhere in evidence, with the Tyrone countryside, with Tulach Oc, Arboe, Lough Neagh.With the site of Tulach Oc, the ambition of a lifetime was realised. May the day be not too far distant when the Gaedheal is again supreme in all that lovely land.' *Seanchas Ard Mhacha*, vol 7, no 2 (1974), p367.
8 C H Crookshank, *History of Methodism in Ireland*, vol 1, 'Wesley and his times' (Belfast 1885).
9 Three people surnamed Armstrong were among the eleven killed at the terrorist bombing of the Remembrance Day service at the Enniskillen Cenotaph in 1987. Neil Armstrong was the American astronaut who first set foot on the moon.
10 From a ballad by Walter Scott of Satchells printed in James Reed, *The Border Ballads* (Stocksfield 1991),p85.

Gallon: a townland in print

W John Bradley

There is a continuing upsurge of interest in the study of townlands and localities. In August 2000, I published my book *Gallon: the history of three townlands in County Tyrone from earliest times to the present day*. In this article I hope to describe my reason for writing the book and suggest an approach to be used and modified by anyone planning to produce a book on their own area.

Telling a book by its cover. Try to convey something of the book's theme or intention with the cover you choose.

Why write a book about Gallon?

Some years ago Dr Bill Crawford invited me to contribute a chapter on the history of Gallon for a book he was editing about townlands in Ulster.[1] I was initially reluctant to agree, fearing that I could not assemble sufficient material on an area which, superficially, appeared to be so similar to other places in Ireland. However, with the help of Dr Crawford and others, I eventually accumulated so much information that not only was I able to provide a chapter for *Townlands in Ulster*, but I decided that there was sufficient to write an entire book on Gallon.

As I proceeded with my research, I realized that I had a number of advantages. Being a native of the place I had a good relationship with the older people who were all willing and eager to provide information. As I had been the last principal of Gallon School I was aware of its records. Furthermore, the fact that I had previously carried out my own research in Gallon during the late 1950s meant that I had original and unique material to work on. In addition I was fortunate in obtaining advice from fellow historians and a generous grant from the Ulster Local History Trust which helped with the cost of publication.

The framework for studying townlands

In *Townlands in Ulster* Dr Crawford suggests a framework which could be used in studying townlands. The framework has nine headings as follows :

- Introduction to the townland
- Location
- History and tradition before the Plantation
- Estates and the creation of farms
- Population growth and decline
- Housing changes
- Changing farm practices
- Development of communications and markets
- The community and its traditions

I found these headings useful and generally adhered to them, while adding one or two of my own!

The framework in action

1. Introduction

Although Gallon is only three miles from the nearest town, Newtownstewart, it still maintains a distinctive identity. This is due perhaps to the existence of Gallon School from 1831 until 1969 which meant that local children stayed longer in their own community, as well as the relative isolation of the area from the outside world before the era of the motor transport. In previous times Gallon children seldom went into Newtownstewart without good reason. When they were not helping with farm work they made their own entertainment in the locality. Meanwhile card playing and ceilidhing in neighbours' houses kept most adults out of the town in the evenings.

Gallon appears on Josiah Bodley's map of the escheated counties of Ulster of about 1609 and it is significant that it is surrounded on three sides by unnamed mountainous areas. It can be identified again at an Inquisition taken at Newtownstewart in 1628 which names townlands in the Plantation 'proportion' of Newtowne and Lislap

....and the severall mountains belonging to the said severall townlands, knowne by the names of Slewtryn and Gallagh a l'Escheeve [Gallon] are the most fitt and convenient of all the aforesaid lands of Newtowne and Lislap, to be graunted and lett to the inhabitants and meere natives of this countrey....[2]

2. Location

It is important that the reader can identify clearly the location of the area being researched. Gallon consists of three townlands, Gallon Upper, Gallon Lower and Gallon Sessiagh. Gallon is about three miles from Newtownstewart, about eight miles from Strabane, and about five miles from Plumbridge.

3. History and tradition before the Plantation

Written information about the Gallon area in the period prior to the Plantation of Ulster has not been discovered. However, there is a wealth of archaeological remains which provide evidence for human life and activity in the area.

In the townlands of Crosh and Glenock, which adjoin Gallon, there are two portal tombs, and cist tombs were unearthed nearby in Shannony East in 1945.

Some years ago a farmer discovered stone walls about a metre below the surface on his farm in Gallon Upper. These walls ran in straight lines for several hundred yards, similar to those which were discovered at the Ceide Fields in Co Mayo. Some time later the charred remains of an ancient fireplace were discovered nearby. These discoveries have been dated to the Neolithic period.

4. Estates and the creation of farms.

The names of some of the Irish families living on the Newtown and Lislap estate in the early seventeenth century are known[3] and many of these names recur in the Gallon census returns three hundred years later. The estate was granted to James Clapham in 1610 but was sold to Sir Robert Newcomen a few years later. Newcomen's son-in-law, William Stewart, rebuilt the town and named it Newtownstewart. Stewart's successors as owners of the estate had the titles Viscount Mountjoy and Earl of Blessington. The Blessington Papers are deposited in the National Library, Dublin. Most of them relate to Dublin and Kilkenny, but there are some papers which deal with the Tyrone properties.

The Blessington properties in County Tyrone were sold in 1846–47 under the Encumbered Estates Act. Daniel Baird, a Derry merchant, bought several townlands, including Gallon Lower and Gallon Upper. In 1852 Baird commissioned R H Nolan to prepare maps of his new estates, and these maps are now deposited in the Public Record Office of Northern Ireland (PRONI).

Charles Edgar Maturin Baird inherited his grand-uncle's lands in 1899. They were eventually sold to the tenant farmers in 1932. Details of the acreage of

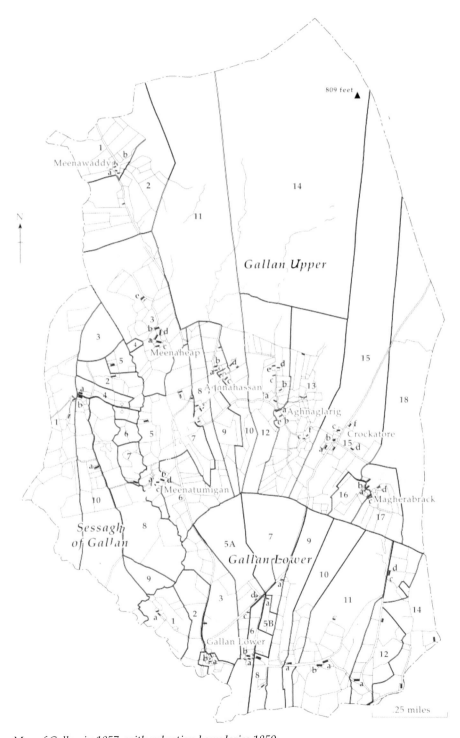

Map of Gallon in 1857, with valuation boundaries 1859.

farms which each tenant bought at this time are recorded in the Land Purchase Commission Records stored at PRONI.

Native Irish families settled permanently in the Gallon area from the time of the Plantation onwards. New farms were established on tracts of more fertile land and many of these locations have particular names, for example, Magherabrack, Meenawiddy, Meenaheap, Meenatumigan and Crockatore. Most of these minor names appear on the Ordnance Survey maps. Many fields in Gallon have their own names. Some of these names are in Irish, often giving information about the field, for example: Clochglare (muddy hill), Crockraffers (prosperous hill), Turnaflochan (hill of the bog cotton), Banshiks (hayfield).

As the population of Gallon increased, it was divided it into three townlands, Gallon Lower, Gallon Upper, and Gallon Sessiagh. The first reference to Gallon Sessiagh as a separate entity is to be found in a marriage settlement for Mary, Lady Tyrawley, daughter of Viscount Mountjoy, which was drawn up around 1696.[4] Another title deed concerns the transfer in 1724 of land from Turlough O'Cregan to Claud Cregan, perhaps in order to prevent a 'popish discovery'.[5] These title deeds can be consulted in the Registry of Deeds in Dublin. In the earlier period leases were applied to entire townlands, but from 1828 onwards there are details of leases for individual farms.

The Tithe Composition Applotment Books for 1834, in PRONI, provide the first complete list of tenant farmers in Gallon, and the Ordnance Survey Memoirs for nearby Ardstraw parish for the same year provide insights into how the people lived. One extract is not particularly flattering:

> The morals of the peasantry are not so good as might be wished. Drunkenness and party spirit still abound to a considerable extent, but cock fighting and private distillation are on the decrease and almost totally confined to the dregs of the people.[6]

5. Population growth and decline

The earliest record of the whole population of Gallon is found in the census returns of 1841. A census of population was held every ten years from 1841 onwards; summaries of these census returns are available from local libraries and from PRONI. The 1901 returns provide the names and particulars of every person living in Gallon at the time and proved exceptionally informative.

In 1958 I carried out a private census of Gallon. In 2000 I arranged for a new census. And in order to fill the gap between 1958 and 1900, I asked an older friend, who had lived all his life in the townland, to make a 'retrospective census' of the population of Gallon in 1935. His findings were verified by other local inhabitants. I used the information from the official and unofficial census returns for 1901, 1935, 1958 and 2000 to provide lists of inhabitants which I included in the book.

Details of baptisms performed at Glenock Roman Catholic Church from 1830

Pat McAnena's house in Gallon Lower, 1996.

until 1880 were also useful, although they did not always give the townland name. I also obtained useful information by studying the gravestones at the old graveyard in the townland of Pubble.

6. Housing changes

There is no specific information regarding housing in Gallon before the Great Famine, but we can assume that most families lived in single roomed cabins. The second General Valuation of Property in Ireland, known as the 'Griffith Valuation', was printed and is accessible through the library system. The volume covering Gallon was published in 1859 and provides the first comprehensive list of all the occupiers of land and houses in Gallon. The Valuation Record books, now in PRONI, were updated annually and illustrate how the size and condition of houses and farms varied over time.

Many houses were still sub-standard up to the end of the 1960s, after which cottiers were re-housed in modern homes in nearby towns and villages. Meanwhile, generous grants were utilized to modernize or replace outdated farmhouses. In 1958 I carried out a survey of housing conditions in Gallon and was able to compare these results with those of a similar survey which was carried out in 2000.

7. Changing farming practices

There is very little specific information on farming practices in the Newtownstewart area before 1800. Nevertheless the existence of an important brown linen market in the town during the second half of the eighteenth century indicates that flax was grown in the surrounding townlands. It has been established that potatoes were first planted in Ulster in the early 1600s, but there is evidence that they did not make an impact in north Tyrone until after 1740. In 1800, John McEvoy, nurseryman on the Newtown and Lislap estate carried out a survey into farming practices in County Tyrone and his resultant book provides valuable information on many aspects of farming and farm development at that time.[7]

The Ordnance Survey Memoirs for the parish of Ardstraw are a useful source of information about farming in the area during the early nineteenth century. Accounts written by visitors and travellers are also worth reading. For example, Jonathan Binns, writing in 1837, had a poor impression of conditions in Tyrone:

> There is no county where the poor are worse off than they are in Tyrone. They evince the strongest anxiety to find work but cannot…. The cabins of the cottiers are mere mud hovels, unfit for the residence of human beings….[8]

The Great Famine of the 1840s caused distress in all parts of Ireland. Workhouses had been opened at Strabane, Gortin and Omagh. Gallon was within the area served by Gortin workhouse, but unfortunately very few records have survived.

Information on crop acreage and domestic animals were collated by the government from 1847 and published in its 'Agricultural Statistics' according to townlands from 1847 until 1857. Thereafter this information was collated according to Electoral Divisions.

From the mid nineteenth century onwards, local newspapers provide useful information on many aspects of life in North Tyrone. The accounts given of Strabane hiring fair are always instructive and often amusing. This one is from an issue of the *Tyrone Constitution* in 1891;

> Farm servants attended in large numbers, but judging by their exhorbitant demands, it is evident that they have little fear of distress or want of employment. Ploughmen are seeking from £6 to £7 for the quarter while boys with a very superficial knowledge of farm work declined to accept £4.10 shillings or £5.10 shillings. Girls were equally exacting….

I found that there were still a few older people who had clear memories of working as a hired boy or girl to farmers, or working on their fathers' farms. The older people in the area were also delighted to reminisce on the social life of the townland in days gone by, including wakes, weddings and parties or 'big nights'. One informant described games which had been played at wakes up to 1945 and which were almost identical to those described by William Carleton in the 1830s.[9]

8. The development of communications, markets and fairs
The first map to show roads to or through Gallon is McCrea and Knox's map

of 1813. The earliest Ordnance Survey map, which appeared in the 1830s, shows the Gallon road running from Glenock church to the Plumbridge – Strabane road complete, but other roads in the townland take somewhat different routes from their modern counterparts.

Details of local markets and fairs are to be found in the archives of the local newspapers, especially the *Ulster Herald* and the *Tyrone Constitution*.

9. The community and its traditions

I found this topic to be the most challenging and yet most rewarding section of my book to prepare. I was already aware of many of the local traditions and this could almost be a disadvantage. However, undertaking research into the area helped me to appreciate the value of traditions which initially I had felt were too inconsequential to mention or which had recently died out of popular usage. I found that my friendship with older residents was particularly valuable in collecting and recording these local traditions.

10. Gallon school

In this chapter I provided a short history of Gallon school, beginning with the applications for grant aid to establish it which had been submitted to the Commissioners of National Education in 1831 and including extracts from Inspectors' Reports into the running of the school from the period 1890-1910.[10]

I was able to reproduce the General Registers of Gallon School from 1896 until 1969. I also included class lists of pupils at intervals of five years from

Teachers and pupils of Gallon School in 1969, the year of its closure. (W J Bradley at back left.)

1918/19 onwards. I also reproduced photographs of school groups taken in 1920, 1926, 1939, 1952 and 1969, and I included many other photographs which I had taken while teaching in the school.

Conclusion

There are many other aspects involved in the publication of a book such as preparation for printing, marketing, and sales, which are important and time consuming. They are dealt with in the contribution made to this volume and our conference by Proinnsíos Ó Duigneáin.

My conclusion is to encourage as many people as possible to undertake research into their localities and townlands while there is still time. It is not enough for local historians simply to know things. We must record them for posterity in an accessible form. The work is important and the need is urgent.

References

1 W H Crawford and R H Foy, *Townlands in Ulster* (Belfast 1998).

2 *Ulster Inquisitions*, Tyrone (5) Car 1. Quoted in Hill, G, *The Plantation of Ulster* (London 1877), p533.

3 Ibid.

4 Registry of Deeds, Dublin Book 56.

5 Registry of Deeds, Dublin Book 95.

6 Angelique Day and Patrick McWilliams (eds), *Ordnance Survey Memoirs of Ireland*, Vol 5, *The Parishes of County Tyrone I* (Belfast 1990).

7 J McEvoy, *A statistical survey of County Tyrone* (Republished Belfast 1991).

8 Day and McWilliams, op. cit.

9 William Carleton, *Traits and Stories of the Irish Peasantry* (Republished Gerrards Cross 1965).

10 *Applications for Grant Aid*, PRONI. ED1/28 and ED 1/30.

Restoring an historic home

Edward O'Kane

Cavanacor House, my home, is situated about one and a half miles from Lifford, just off the main Lifford to Letterkenny road. The border and the town of Strabane are clearly visible from the house.

Cavanacor House is one of the oldest inhabited houses in County Donegal. It was built in the early 1600s by Roger Tasker who came to Lifford as a lieutenant to Sir Richard Hansard, who was in charge of the Plantation in that area. Cavanacor was built for strategic reasons on high ground overlooking a crossing point on the River Deele.

On 20 April 1689, at the time of the Siege of Derry, King James II had a meal under a large sycamore tree on the lawn in front of Cavanacor. He gave the house protection, which saved it from being burned when his troops withdrew from Derry after the lifting of the siege.

The original builder of Cavanacor had two daughters called Barbara and Magdalen. The house was given to Barbara as part of her marriage portion when she married John Keys, and it became the main seat of the Keys family in Ireland from that point. The younger daughter, Magdalen, married firstly a Captain Porter. On his death, she married Robert Bruce Pollock, an officer from Porter's regiment. In the 1680s Magdalen and her husband emigrated to the American colony of Maryland. After their arrival in America, their name was shortened to 'Polk'. Her great-great-great-grandson was James Knox Polk, eleventh President of the United States. This means that we have a remarkable situation where the ancestral homes of two American Presidents of Ulster origin face each other across the border. From our front door at Cavanacor we can look across to President Woodrow Wilson's ancestral home above Strabane. Both Polk and Wilson were 'War Presidents'.[1]

Cavanacor House.

When my wife and I bought Cavanacor in 1974, we were aware that the house had a history, but we did not appreciate the degree of its interest and extent. Since then I have studied the families associated with the house. In so doing I have been fortunate to have access to primary source documentation in the form of indentures, wills and marriage contracts which trace the house back to the 1600s.

Cavanacor is in the area where, in the sixteenth century, the territories of the important Gaelic families of O'Neill and O'Donnell met. In 1600, shortly before the building of the house, a battle had taken place at the river crossing at Tyleford between the O'Donnells and the English garrison at Lifford. The proximity of the house to the Donegal/Tyrone border and the strategic reasons for its building on a site overlooking an important river crossing have made its immediate surroundings a scene of contention for many hundreds of years. Nevertheless it remained in the hands of the descendants of the original builder until the 1960s, passing at various times through the female line with the owners' name changing from Tasker to Keys to Humfrey.

The present property comprises ten and a half acres. The walled garden is several hundred years old and is mentioned in the original deeds of the house from the early 1600s. It contains many interesting and rare plants, including *rosa rugosa*, *rosa mundi*, moss roses, oriental poppies, with a rare pink poppy, double headed snowdrops, and early varieties of daffodils.

The house has been in continuous habitation since it was built. When we bought it the water supply was from a deep stone-lined well at the back. During our first year we connected to the water mains and rewired the house. However, while the house was in habitable condition, the outbuildings and surrounding parkland were very run down. Over the next decade we set about restoring the outbuildings and gardens. In the initial stages, we found the lack of finances frustrating. In time, we realised that it is very important to get to know a property well before making irreversible changes. Much harm can be done through insensitive and ill-informed restoration. I carried out research into buildings of the period and

In the garden, Cavanacor.

Outbuilding restored to serve as art gallery and tea-room.

discovered that the layout of the outbuilding at the top of the yard was similar to that of 'Devon long houses' of the 1600s.

This building had previously had part of its roof removed in the 1960s to save money on rates. We photographed and recorded the existing structure and took measurements of all the salient features. We received funding from the International Fund for Ireland to restore the building to include a gallery, tea room and craft shop. A local stonemason rebuilt the collapsed section of the building and carpenters who had worked in the Ulster American Folk Park made doors and sliding sash windows. The flag stone floor was in poor state and very uneven. We retained some of the flags and replaced others with Donegal flagstones. I spent a whole summer sourcing second-hand Bangor blue slates for the building which required complete re-roofing.

We are now in the position where many of the other outbuildings require urgent work to be carried out on the roofs. Some of these are rare hipped roofs with graded slates. Many of these slates were secured with wooden pegs that have now rotted. While makeshift repairs have been carried out, much damage is being caused by incoming water. We have the expertise and knowledge of old buildings which makes us aware of the possibility and potential afforded by correct restoration. Unfortunately, we lack the funds to carry out this necessary work.

Cavanacor House has been recognised by the Office of Public Works in the Irish Republic as a building of outstanding national historic importance. We have had many thousands of visitors from all over the world. Tourists, schools, historical societies, and special interest groups have all shared in the unique history of Cavanacor. However, we have received no state funding whatsoever to help with the restoration. I believe that families such as ours are unsupported custodians of our history and that a radical reappraisal of heritage policy is needed before more of the historic fabric of the country is lost forever. While I realise that the responsible authorities are restricted by the budget allocated to them, I believe that a much more proactive and supportive approach is needed to address the problem. Historic homes such as ours continue to have their own life and can be compared in value to museums. They are not dead objects if they have owners who are willing to identify contemporary usage for such buildings which will complement their unique nature and benefit from the setting.

Cavanacor remains very much a family house although several rooms are open to the public and contain furniture and paintings from 1600-1800. Because my wife and myself and our six children are all involved in artistic pursuits we decided, in the past two years, to concentrate on the provision of an art gallery. This now brings artists of national and international importance to the northwest. This venture has drawn on our own particular strengths and experience. I am a trained painter and my wife Joanna a trained sculptress. Our daughter Marianne is a lecturer on the Visual Arts in Ireland on Boston University's Internship Programme in Dublin. She is the curator of Cavanacor Gallery. Our son Eamon, who is also a painter, has had solo exhibitions in many countries worldwide. In addition to our own work, we have had solo shows in Cavanacor Gallery by Belfast based Neil Shawcross and Rosaleen Davey and Mick O'Dea from Dublin. Our group shows have included Denise Ferran, Felim Egan, Brian Ballard, Sean Fingleton and Michael Kane. Svend Bruun from Denmark, April Kinser from America, and Anita Taylor from England with many others have also exhibited. The gallery has achieved national and international recognition. People are prepared to travel from Belfast and Dublin to appreciate and purchase art at Cavanacor.

In 1974 we thought we acquired an historic home. In fact, the historic home acquired myself and my family as custodians for the rest of our lives. The Irish have a valuable heritage residing in historic homes and gardens throughout the country. Without realistic support from Government funding agencies much of this heritage will disappear in the near future.

Acknowledgment

1 I am indebted to Annesley Malley, another participant in this conference, who drew my attention to research material in his possession which, together with my own research, brought to light the link between Cavanacor and President Polk.

How to write Local History

John Lynch

If you think about it the title of my paper gives me a fairly impossible task. I can not possibly cover everything. It is a bit like the evening I was asked to give a lecture on Irish history from the Stone Age to the seventeenth century. All I can offer are fairly general guidelines and I apologise if I insult anybody's intelligence. That is not my intention. However I am assuming that I am addressing those who wish to begin writing, as well as those who already are, so please bear with me. I am also making a major assumption, with which I hope you agree. I believe that local history is a legitimate and valid form of history, not some sort of eccentric hobby practised by the strange and outlandish. Therefore I would argue that the local historian must accept the same standards in terms of research and presentation of data as any other historian. There can be no half-measures. Local or specialist studies are simply too important.

Introduction
- Why do we write history? There are many, often contradictory, reasons but arguably all are based on a desire to pass on research and ideas.
- Why do we not write?
  1. Often we may feel that what we have to offer is not 'important'.
  2. Personal insecurity; 'I am not worthy'.
  3. Fear of criticism; *'They* will talk about me'.
  4. Somebody else will do it, so why should I?
- How can these quite legitimate and almost universal fears be overcome?
  1. Recognise the role of the local study; it is unique and critically important.
  2. Realise that *all* writers can feel insecure and unworthy.
  3. Realise that criticism in various forms can be positive and constructive.
  4. Never assume that somebody else will write the history, and remember that no other individual can bring your unique insight and experience to a project.

Step One: Assembling your resources
- Take time to think about and list the libraries, archives, publications, and other sources of relevant information. Do not rush this stage; it is absolutely critical to avoid reinventing the wheel in research terms.
- Talk to others who have worked on similar projects. Every researcher has their pet horror stories and can offer invaluable personal experience. Most of those who work in history are happy to talk to others and such

advice is invaluable.

- Arrange a literature search or spend time in the catalogue of a good reference library. Look critically at what has already been written - how can it be improved? Is there a need for a complete reappraisal? Do not be put off by several books on the same or related topics. You can be different.
- At this stage think about the type of questions you are seeking to answer, who, what, why, where, or any of the others. You can set out to answer a single problem or weave several into your text.

Step Two: The Focusing Exercise

You will reach a certain point where you will know what you want to write about and where you can get the information. Then you must focus yourself on the activity of writing.

- Think very carefully about what you think you want to write about. Ideally write a short synopsis to concentrate your thoughts (200-300 words). Remember this will probably not match exactly what you end up writing. It seldom does, so do not worry if you wander off your self-laid track.
- Recognise your limitations. Ask yourself if writing the 'Complete History of Everything' in one volume is practical. On a more serious level you need to balance ambition - what you would like to do - against reality - what you can or are allowed to do. This may be slightly frustrating but is best accomplished at this stage.
- Read the literature, become completely familiar with what has already been written, not only will this save you time and effort by avoiding repetition of research already done by others but it also feeds ideas and views into you project.
- Set yourself reasonable deadlines. It is all too easy to become engrossed in a project and keep working at it for ever. Set yourself a completion date. Nevertheless, remember you are setting the rules and you have the right to break them if you see fit. It's not the end of the world. But I would ask you to remember the words of Alice Ellis:

  I believe if I were locked in a windowless room with a deadline I would spend the time trying to tunnel out rather than get on with it.

- Seriously ask yourself why you are doing this book. The reasons can be as various as the authors - money, fame, the overthrow of capitalism, etcetera, etcetera, but it is very useful to work out your own agenda before beginning.

Step Three: Designing what goes in

Research is often much easier if you decide in advance what style and format your publication is going to take. It saves both wasted hours in the archives and panics at the end. What can or should a good history contain?

- Illustrated histories are both attractive and accessible. Consider the effective use of photographs and maps, but do not just dump them into the text on their own; they need to be fully integrated.

- Statistical data is invaluable to the local historian, although I'm fully aware how frightening figures are to many people. Good data presented in the form of tables or graphics can often add factual 'meat' to a narrative.

- There used to be a school of local history that dismissed references as 'academic' and not to be used by writers who sought to appeal to the 'ordinary person'. In fact all this did was spoil otherwise excellent local material by making it impossible in too many cases to confirm authors findings or conclusions or check the sources employed.

- A bibliography of materials used is vital. You will be amazed how much you will cover. Once you start researching you will quickly come to realise just how useful such material can be for others. Always share your knowledge and experience.

- Organise your material around an introductory chapter and a conclusion. These are really quite separate and very useful pieces. The *Introduction* serves to define exactly what you are writing about, and is often actually the last bit of a thesis or book to be written. You should state exactly what aspects of history you cover and explain why you may have taken a conscious decision not to consider some issues. In short you inform the public, and potential critics, of the agenda you intend to cover. If the *Conclusion* is well written it should summarise, not repeat, your arguments and findings from the body of the work. It should be possible to grasp the broad outline of a work from the conclusion. This is difficult to write well but it is a skill worth cultivating.

Step Four: Creating a Working Environment

If you are going to write you need somewhere where you can do so. This sounds obvious - but think about it. The dining table may offer sufficient space but others wish to use it! Imagine just reaching a peak of creative energy and being told to clear the table because dinner is almost ready. Will you ever recapture that moment? You need a spot where you can work undisturbed and where the clutter of activity will not offend others or seriously interfere in their lifestyle; a spare bedroom, the attic, a garden shed, the back of the garage, anywhere in fact where you can work undisturbed. If you are by nature a tidy person you may find the experience of writing something of a culture shock, you may well find yourself living in mess as Maureen Lipman explained rather well:

> I work in chaos. My desk, as I survey it from my vantage point, looks like a still life from Hieronymus Bosch.

Is this negative? I would argue that it is not. For some people mess is in fact a feature of the creative process as Katherine Whitehorn noted:

> The more a thing is filed away, the more totally useless it is. A sweet disorder in

the desk at least ensures that the whole thing is ploughed through often enough for useful things to come to the surface.

I work in a perpetual state of untidiness. If I am writing a lecture or article a nest like ring of books, articles and notes slowly builds around my chair and I make no apology for this either to you or the frustrated cleaners at Queen's University. If this method works for you, live in peace with your mess. But remember that you must not force it upon others who do not share your passion. Remember that writing should be a pleasurable experience for many reasons, as Lynne Truss pointed out:

> The main advantage of working at home is that you get to find out what cats really do all day.

Step Five: The loneliness of the long-distance author

Once you begin writing you will find yourself confronted with a strange physical and mental process that any author can recognise and from which we have all suffered at various times. Let us start by considering some of the common crises you will face and consider methods of overcoming the difficulties these create:

- There is the 'Why did I ever start this' mood, when the whole project seems to have ground to a halt and nothing you can do seems capable of shifting it any further.

  Almost inevitably this is caused by simple mental exhaustion. You try too hard to get something finished and feel increasing frustration. There really is only one answer. Take a break. Either put the whole thing away for a couple of weeks or, even better, work on something completely different! You will be surprised how interesting the material you have written will be when you return to it.

- There is the 'I can't find anything on this subject' crisis where suddenly the location or person you are researching seems to vanish from the records. Did you imagine them?

  Often in the early stages of research you find lots of material and quickly build up a mass of information. However, once the obvious sources are fully worked the process slows down dramatically. This means that you are now looking for less obvious data in less well explored areas. You may be finding less but the quality of the material obtained is often far higher.

- There is the 'I'll never meet the deadline/finish this thing' syndrome. Every time you look at the project there seems to be more than ever to do!

  Again this is often caused by sheer exhaustion in the later stages of a project. A bit like running a marathon, the last few miles all seem to get progressively longer. Also this can be caused by unreal expectations. Are you setting yourself an unrealistic target that simply cannot be achieved?

- There is the 'This is not what I started' panic, when you suddenly realise that what you are producing is quite different from what you first envisaged.

  In fact this is not a problem, quite the opposite. This is a perfectly natural process and a good research project will shift and adapt to make full use of the material you have. This is not a sign of failure, rather an indicator of real success.

Any author needs support mechanisms. To try any work entirely on your own is not just counter productive but also potentially harmful, both to yourself and your relationships to those about you. This support can take a number of forms:

- A member of your family or a particularly close friend to whom you can boast/scream/moan as the work progresses and who will not turn round and say something like 'Come on! It's not that important.' Value the highly necessary, and seldom adequately acknowledged, 'soggy shoulder'. If you are ever called upon to act in this role I beg you to remember the words of the publisher Michael Joseph; "Authors are easy to get on with – if you like children."

- An honest critic, somebody who will read your material and tell you its strengths and weakness without trying to protect your feelings. This has to be somebody whose judgement you trust and respect and whom you value sufficiently not to fall out with when they point out mistakes. Again, if called upon to carry out this role be sensitive, if for no other reason than because your hour will come. Avoid comments such as Anthony Hope Hawkins on J.M. Barrie's *Peter Pan*; "Oh for the hour of Herod."

- A sounding board, at a certain point you must present your work to a wider audience for criticism or comment. This is always a difficult moment but it is vital to the process. A good local history society is invaluable as a well-informed test bench - traumatic but necessary. Remember critics all have their personal views and prejudices. As George Nathan pointed out they would be useless without them; "Show me a critic without prejudices, and I'll show you an arrested cretin."

- A competent doctor/psychologist/councillor/minister of religion. Just remember this is a highly stressful activity. Particularly if you fear criticism on the level of L S Klepp's infamous article in *Entertainment Weekly*:

  A reviewer is obligated to point out typographical errors, no matter how trivial. In the 'about the author' note at the end of the book, we are told 'Roy Blount, Jr is a novelist. Now.' This makes sense only if the errant 'w' at the end of the last word is omitted. Apart from this bit of inadvertent humour, *First Hubby* is flawlessly lame.

Finally I feel I must warn you of some common irritations that have probably plagued historians from the earliest days of the subject and which you will all have faced or will face.

- There is the individual who says something like, 'I've got stuff on that and I'll pass it on.' Do not hold your breath or rely on this; in all too many cases it never appears.
- There is the even less helpful person who says 'I'm sure somebody has already written on that subject' but of course cannot remember the author, the name of the book or when it was published. Odds on the imagined book never existed but this certainly undermines your confidence.
- The 'friend' who offers to read your material or asks to look at something you are working on and then announces "I've lost your notes/manuscript/illustrations. Do you have another copy?" All I would advise is to try and avoid actual physical violence, or at least to hit them where the bruises will not show in court.
- My pet hate is the maggot who looks at your work and says something completely dismissive like, "Good ideas here but not up to academic standards are they," and fails to offer any valid suggestions for improvement. Bluntly, that is snobbery of the worst kind and such individuals and their opinions deserve to be ignored. Unfortunately from personal experience I know just how demoralising they can be.

Conclusion

There is a danger that I might have put many potential historians off the idea. After this talk that computer course does seem even more attractive? However, I would simply say this. I find researching and writing on the past an immensely interesting and satisfying activity and hope that as many others as possible can come to appreciate it. In recent years I have taught Local Studies at Queens University in Belfast and have sought to create a programme which not only describes the past but also seeks to show students how historians work and how our views of the past are created. I regard that as a legitimate activity of a historian, although I understand some of my colleagues are a bit sick of students who have passed through my hands continually asking 'Who?', Why?', and 'Who For?', when confronted with documents or readings.

I have not covered everything. I warned you I could not, but don't be afraid to ask any questions you might have. Participating in conferences and meetings such as this one on 'The Debateable Land' will bring you into contact with other working historians whose views and methods may differ from mine. Talk to them too and make use of all of us.

Publishing on the Border

Proinnsíos Ó Duigneáin

Drumlin Publications of Manorhamilton, County Leitrim, of which I am Managing Director, was established in 1989. To date it has been involved in about thirty publications, mainly in local history. These have included parish histories and church histories such as that of Dromahaire, or Drumcliffe Church of Ireland, and family accounts like Ó Ruairc of Breifne. We have produced *North Leitrim in Land League Times*, biographies, and books of wide interest such as *Between the jigs and the reels – the Donegal fiddle tradition*.

At the present time, 2001, we are at different stages in the production of three biographies of local people; Sir Frederick Hamilton, founder of Manorhamilton; Linda Kearns, Sligo revolutionary and nurse; and of Seán Mac Diarmada, one of the leaders of the 1916 Rising. We are also working on a book of poems in Irish by Seán Ó Coistealbha with English translations by well known writers.

In most respects publishing local history on a small scale should be no different to publishing at the national level, except perhaps in one important respect - the print run. I will come to that later. However it has to be admitted that, in the past, the editing and production standards of local works sometimes left a lot to be desired. There is no excuse for this and it is important for the local publisher to pay particular attention to the following processes.

Editing

1. Editing involves putting yourself in the position of the potential reader. An editor is not unlike the director of a play interpreting, refining, and filtering the material for public consumption.

2. The editor eradicates repetition and errors of fact. Some knowledge of the subject is very important.

3. The editor makes sure that the text is properly organised and punctuated. Don't assume that even the most knowledgeable author can always spell correctly.

3. Editing often requires consultation with the author. Some of the sentences may be too long or confusing and even whole sections may have to be rewritten, put in a different order, or omitted. In our experience most authors are happy to co-operate in teasing out the problems.

4. The editor will ensure that the book follows a coherent theme with each chapter or section building up to a complete whole.

5. Photographs and illustrations should be positioned to best advantage in the text. After all, they are there to enhance the narrative, not to be lumped in a separate corner of their own.

7. A recognised method of referencing and an index are essential for works of local history.

Design

A professional should be employed for the design and layout of the text. The cover is very important. Laminate it to preserve it. The designer should read the work; they may be inspired by something in the text. The author should also be consulted about the cover. The title should be carefully thought out. Our most recent book, relating to women's lives in Glenfarne, Co Leitrim from 1920 to1960, is called *Rinso Days and Rainbow Nights* and this title has proved eye-catching.

Printing

Approach three or four printers for written quotations, and put your precise requirements to them in writing also. It is very important that you ask them all to quote for the same thing (same size, same type of paper etc), otherwise you have no 'benchmark' against which to evaluate their responses, as well as demonstrating that you have not thought out your own requirements properly.

Printing costs in Ireland are quite high and some Irish books are produced as far away as China. However, orders have to be placed months in advance of the launch date if you go down this road. We have never printed overseas as we find that, as in any other business, it is important to build up personal relationships. A good relationship with your printer may be very useful if a deadline is looming and things are not going to plan! On the other hand you must pay attention to value for money and realise that competition in the printing industry in Ireland is growing. In the long run this will benefit the local publisher.

Marketing and publicity

When deciding on the selling price of your book it is important to do the sums carefully and remember that bookshops will take at least 35% of the marked price of the book. Some are looking for 40%. If the book is marketed by a national distributor the cost is at least 50% of the retail price. Remember to count the designer's fee and all other costs, as well as the cost of printing, before deciding on the price.

It is extremely important to get as much free publicity as possible. This can be achieved through local notes in newspapers, in parish bulletins, on local radio and in the local history section of some national newspapers. A well organised launch can be extremely important to send the book on its way. Invite a well-known personality to do the launch and try to get it sponsored. Send review copies to local and national papers, and in some cases it may also be effective to send some overseas.

The cost and the print run

Funding arrangements for your book will depend on many factors. Assuming you are publishing it on a voluntary basis, rather than having it done for you by another publisher, you should consider if it merits local sponsorship. Some publications may be eligible for grant-aid through various schemes for cultural or community development or through the Arts Councils, north and south. Explore the ground carefully, but if you don't need financial assistance, don't ask for it.

In our experience in the Irish Republic, the cost of a paperback of approximately 150 pages, on average, is about 6350 Euro for a print run of 1500/2000 copies. The decision on the number of copies to print is the most difficult for any publisher. It is said that the one of the busiest machines in big international publishing houses is the shredder! Obviously for the local publisher, for whom the unit cost is the same, shredding is not an option. We have found that 1500 copies will sell out in two to three years except in exceptional circumstances.

Dos and don'ts for the local history publisher

Don't accept the work, and don't give it to a printer, unless it is on computer disk.

Don't end up writing the book yourself! We have had experience of local historians telling us, "Sure I'll give you the material and you can put it together yourself."

Don't be pressurised into thinking you really must publish a particular book because it is so significant. You can only publish within the limits of your resources.

Do tell yourself every day, "I will never again try to publish a book to coincide with the imminent official opening of a sports ground or to celebrate the dedication of a church due to take place next Sunday three weeks!"

Do remind yourself frequently that you are doing a very important job!

Roddy Hegarty at the Federation for Ulster Local Studies bookstall.

The plight of Monaghan Protestants, 1911-26

Terence Dooley

During the inter-censal period 1911 to 1926, the Protestant population of County Monaghan declined by 23 per cent. This fact, perhaps more than any other, illustrates the great effect which the political, social and, indeed, economic upheavals of this period had upon the Protestant community. To put this decline into perspective, the population of the Roman Catholic community in the county fell by only 4 per cent during the same period.

From 1880 to 1911, the dominant political and socio-economic position of the Protestant community in the county had been under attack. During the last quarter of the nineteenth century, political ascendancy had been virtually obliterated at both national and local levels by the growth of the Home Rule movement which drew its support from an ever expanding Catholic and nationalist electorate. From the 1880 general election, the hold of the county's Protestant landed families on parliamentary representation was broken. Almost two decades later, the Local Government of Ireland Act of 1898 established a County Council to replace the old grand jury system. The members of the Council from 1899 onwards were predominantly Catholic and nationalist as were the members of urban and rural district councils; Protestants therefore lost all political influence at local level.

However, the political machinery of the Protestant community by no means ground to a halt. If anything it was reinvigorated by the third Home Rule crisis of 1912. Although the third Home Rule Bill offered Ireland only a narrow measure of autonomy, it was vehemently opposed by unionists both north and south. Monaghan Protestants enthusiastically supported the unionist cause. They joined locally established Unionist Clubs (affiliated to the Ulster Unionist Council since its establishment in 1905) and in September 1912, 5,000 Monaghan Protestant males signed the Ulster Solemn League and Covenant. By August 1913 there were at least 1,200 members of the Ulster Volunteer Force in the county, divided into two battalions, led by local landlords and Protestant professional men and organised from the beginning through local Orange lodges.

By July 1914, the UVF were in possession of at least 1,700 rifles which had come into the county following the Larne gun-running of April of that year, and which were stored in big houses throughout the county as well as in Orange halls and even Protestant schools and rectories. Monaghan Protestants, it seems, were prepared to oppose the implementation of Home Rule by force if necessary.

Ostentatious displays of military style training by the UVF incensed local nationalists who from April 1914 flocked to the Irish National Volunteers. By the end of that summer there were in excess of 5,000 Irish Volunteers in the county. Bitter sectarian feeling began to surface in certain areas as the county's population became more polarised along politico-religious lines. Nationalists saw the introduction of Home Rule as a means of fulfilling their aspirations of breaking down the remaining vestiges of Protestant power in the county, while unionists saw its defeat as the only means by which to safeguard their remaining rights. While a degree of sectarian bitterness had always existed in the county this was the first time that it threatened to manifest itself openly in armed conflict since 1641. However, the outbreak of the Great War in August 1914 defused the situation. Nevertheless the war had significant long-term consequences for the Protestant community of Monaghan.

Before discussing these consequences, it should first be pointed out that Protestants in the county did not join the British forces in the same numbers or with the same enthusiasm as they did in the more industrialised and urbanised areas of Ulster. In fact, Protestant recruitment in Monaghan was very poor. Probably the main reason for this was the fact that most Protestant families in the county were engaged in agriculture and the rapid rise in agricultural profits during the war years was much more of an incentive to stay at home than go to the front. This fact was certainly not lost on many of the unionist leaders who became very critical of the contribution of Protestant farmers' sons to the war effort.

This poor contribution from the farming community drove a wedge between the unionist leaders and the rank and file, with the former being unable to empathise with the apathy of the latter towards recruitment. The leaders could not be accused of apathy; they concentrated wholeheartedly on the war effort to the exclusion of local unionist organisation, with the result that by the time the war was over the unionist movement in the county, and indeed the Orange Order, had fallen greatly into decline. The fact that a large number of prominent pre-war leaders either died of natural causes from 1914 to 1918 or, like Norman Leslie and Gerald Madden, were killed at the front, meant that by the end of the war, the Protestant community was deprived of many of its former or potential leaders. Finally, as a result of the Buckingham Palace conference of July 1914, Lloyd George's attempts towards a settlement of the Home Rule question in 1916, and the Irish Convention of 1917-18, the war years led to an acceptance in some influential Ulster Unionist circles that partition was inevitable.

By 1920, the Ulster Unionist Council had come to see the merits of a six-county split. In March of that year it unanimously rejected a resolution from the unionists of Monaghan, Cavan and Donegal to "take such steps as may be necessary to see that the term Northern Ireland in the permanent bill is altered to include the whole province of Ulster."

This so-termed partition crisis ushered in the second and perhaps most important phase in the decline of unionism in Monaghan because it ultimately left the county under the jurisdiction of a Dublin government, in a Free State in which unionism had no place. The alienation of local Protestant leaders from their unionist principles as a result of their abandonment by the UUC meant that the rank and file were now virtually leaderless, disorganised and unable to cope with the attacks directed against them during the growing Anglo-Irish conflict.

From 1917, the rise of Sinn Fein in the county signalled the beginning of the growth of a new and more violent form of sectarian bitterness which was to manifest itself in outrages directed against the Protestant community between

1919 and 1923. The War of Independence in the county was fought very much along sectarian lines. The local IRA were faced not only with the Black and Tans and Auxiliaries but also with a fifth column of Protestants organised in various localities as Protestant Defence Associations. The involvement of many IRA volunteers in sectarian crimes may be partially explained by the existence and influence of ancestral grievances. Similarly, the success of the Belfast Boycott in County Monaghan, aimed primarily at the local Protestant business community, suggests that it was used as a pretext to break the economic hold of Protestant businesses in towns such as Clones, Castleblayney and Monaghan itself.

The ending of the Civil War in May 1923 effectively ended the outward display of sectarian bitterness directed against Protestants. But this was largely because the revolutionary years had resulted in the final demise of unionist politics in Monaghan and satisfied to a great extent nationalist aspirations of gaining a firmer grip of the political, social and commercial life of the county. Indeed, the revolutionary years had also led to a high rate of Protestant migration from the county to Northern Ireland. From 1919 to 1925, 454 Protestants had migrated from Monaghan to Fermanagh alone, the highest rates of migration being from rural border areas and towns such as Clones which were most adversely affected by the War of Independence and the Belfast Boycott.

Those Protestants who remained in the county after independence, particularly those living in the border areas, looked to the promised Boundary Commission to transfer them to Northern Ireland. They presented themselves to the Boundary Commission in community groups, committees and as individuals to plead their cases for the transfer of their respective areas to Northern Ireland. Most were careful to base their reasons on economic and geographical factors, but some could not hide their political preferences to 'live under the Union Jack' once again. Of course, these last burning embers of unionist sentiment (or perhaps, more accurately. continued loyalism) amongst Monaghan Protestants rekindled some of the fire in local nationalists who felt obliged to submit counter (or what were referred to as negative) claims. Their claims more than anything else illustrate the political undertones which were present for they show that while Catholic farmers and businessmen suffered the same inconveniences as their Protestant neighbours, they were quite willing to put up with them in order to remain under the jurisdiction of the Free State.

The publication of the Boundary Commission's recommendations, rather conveniently leaked to the ultra-conservative *Morning Post* caused such a furore that they were never implemented. Monaghan nationalists, determined to safeguard the county's territorial boundaries, sacrificed boundary changes that might very well have prevented Monaghan becoming an economic cul-de-sac in the long term. As it was the border came to be the dividing line between the industrialised economy of Northern Ireland on the one side and a relatively underdeveloped economy in the South. Economically, Monaghan began a rapid decline, symbolised by its designation as an underdeveloped region in 1952. And if Monaghan Protestants wanted to become part of Northern Ireland, they had only one option left - migration. It was an option many were to avail of in the decades ahead.

Investigative History: a case study Lord Farnham and the 'Second Reformation'

Myrtle Hill

What are we doing when we set out to research the past? No doubt we intend to inform ourselves about our locality and the individuals and communities who inhabited it. But does that just mean gathering the facts? What if the 'facts' are debated and disputed – the subject of controversy and disagreement? If there are several different versions of events – not an unusual occurrence in Northern Ireland - whose 'truth' do we accept? This paper will discuss some of the challenges involved in historical reconstruction and analysis, stressing the need to be aware of the reasons behind people's actions, and the relationships between particular actions and the wider context. The relationship between individuals and the wider community, and the implications and consequences of actions, also need to be taken into account.

The task of the historian is not unlike that of the detective. We need to search for clues and make ourselves aware of the background of the various protagonists and their personalities, concerns and relationships. While secondary writings can help fill us in on the social, religious and political background, primary materials can be scrutinized for more direct evidence. Personal letters and estate files, pamphlet literature, and both local and national newspapers are particularly helpful in this regard.

The example I will use to discuss these issues is the controversy surrounding an apparent outbreak of religious conversions in County Cavan in the 1820s, which came to be known as the Second Reformation. The original Reformation, as most people will be aware, aimed to reform the Roman Catholic Church and resulted in the founding of Protestant Churches. It made very limited progress in Ireland. During the late 1820s, however, many Protestants were claiming that enough conversions to Protestantism had taken place to justify the claim that a 'second reformation' was underway. The spotlight fell particularly on County Cavan where, amidst the claims and counter claims of religious conversions, the local peasantry was apparently caught in a power struggle between the Catholic religious hierarchy and Protestant evangelicals.[1]

John Maxwell Barry, Lord Farnham 1823-38, who owned some 29,000 acres in the county, and was a powerful political influence both locally and nationally,[2] was deeply implicated in the controversy. It began with his claim that three Roman Catholic schoolmasters in Cavan had publicly rejected their faith and converted to Protestantism. He asserted that, following this, on 8th October 1826, seventeen people had gathered at the local parish church to renounce their Catholic faith. Two weeks later they were followed by twenty more converts and, claimed Farnham, Catholics continued to 'turn' to the Protestant faith at the rate of about thirty a week.[3] By 6th January 1827, it was claimed that there were 450 converts in County Cavan alone.

How do we account for this seemingly spontaneous wave of conversions? Clearly, such incidents generate their own momentum, and the air of religious excitement was to some extent self-perpetuating. The effective publicity machine put into action by evangelical Protestants to monitor the 'Progress of the Reformation' also accelerated enthusiasm. Information on the number of converts was prominently displayed on walls and gables, and men were employed to parade around the streets with similar statistics on billboards round their necks.[4] Evangelical newspapers across Ireland and England were also quick to capitalize on the emotion and drama surrounding these events.

Not surprisingly, both the claims themselves, and the massive publicity surrounding them, caused considerable alarm amongst the Roman Catholic hierarchy. Such was the concern that a high-level deputation, consisting of the Archbishop of Armagh and four other bishops, was sent to Cavan to find out exactly what was happening. On their arrival in the town, however, the bishops were immediately confronted by itinerant Protestant preachers who publicly challenged their religious authority. Despite noisy exchanges and heckling from the crowd, the deputation continued its investigations into the claims of mass conversions, with the bishops finally announcing themselves unimpressed either by the number of converts or their character. They argued that they could only verify about forty-two individual conversions, of people aged between eight and sixty,[5] and added,

> if names and places be specified … it will be found that many of the new converts are old Protestants, and that others are such as to make every decent Protestant blush for his new allies.[6]

They argued that those amongst the Catholic peasantry who had converted were merely responding pragmatically to hunger and hardship, and that they fell easily under the influence of their apparently benevolent landlord, who publicly welcomed them into the Protestant religion. Tenants were, after all, mostly concerned with trying to keep their homes and their jobs and, as G K Ensor put it, "misery acquaints us with strange bedfellows". The converts were like birds, he said,

> which visit milder climates at intervals – but their coming is proof of a great severity in their native country, and they return when the iron days are passed and the sun cheers them from home.[7]

The Catholic clergy insisted that the entire story was one of 'systematic deception', a combination of 'fraud and force', and they refused to engage with the Protestant evangelists who challenged them to public debate.

On their part, the Protestant camp denounced the Catholic claims as 'a tissue of the grossest falsehoods'. Lord Farnham, who was particularly suspected of bribing his tenants to convert, passionately objected. He said none of the converts were his immediate tenants (a claim hotly disputed), and that no rewards were given for recantation.[8] Nonetheless, despite his protestations, he was personally the subject of scepticism, derision and scorn in the wider Catholic community:

A pious yell doth smite the air,
With note like bugle call;
Inviting converts to repair
With speed to Farnham Hall.
The Moral Agents sally forth
And cry throughout the land,
'Come all ye vagrants of the north,
salvation is at hand'.[9]

At this stage, it would perhaps be helpful to take a look at Farnham's estate and how it was managed. Farnham took over the 29,000 acre estate in 1823. In *A Statement of the Management of the Farnham Estates*, drawn up in 1830 in response to the requests of local proprietors, he explained the foundation of the system he had introduced.[10] He stated that, "the principles upon which it is built up are, as far as may be, in strict compliance with the precepts and spirit of the Holy Book." To facilitate its 'moral management', the estate was divided into five districts. Each was overseen by a land and a moral agent under the 'friendly supervision' of an inspectorate. The relation between landlord and tenant was to be one of mutual goodwill and dependence. The landlord would provide churches, day schools, Sunday schools, a lending library, and material aid for those who earned it. The tenant was expected to be responsive to this liberality. Punctual payment of rent, for example, was considered beneficial to both parties, and the employment of the much-hated 'drivers' was thus rendered unnecessary.[11]

The moral agent was the mainspring of the whole system. The appointment of a worthy individual to the position was a major anxiety for evangelical landlords concerned with the spiritual welfare of their tenantry.[12] Lord Farnham's moral agent between 1826 and 1838 was William Krause.[13] Born in the West Indies in 1796, but living in England from an early age, Krause had undergone a classic religious conversion after a dangerous illness ended his army career. The position in Cavan was felt by both employer and employee to be just right for one preparing for the ministry and the pastoral duties it entailed. Krause, who was ordained as curate in Cavan in 1838, availed himself of every opportunity to expound to large congregations on the estate. He fully supported the system, of which he became a crucial component, recognizing the task as one of "trying to free Roman Catholics from bondage". He regretted that many other gentry were "too afraid of persecution" to follow a similar course.

It was with the moral agent that tenants had the most frequent contact. Besides his practical duties of removing paupers and supervising schools and buildings, it was through him that all requests of the tenantry were passed. He in turn reported their conditions to the inspectors and land agent. On principle, he was kept apart from the whole area of rent collection, and was expected to be "continually urging and exhorting the tenantry".

The system professed to heighten the individual responsibility of the tenants by cutting out middlemen and coercion. But the emphasis – indeed insistence – on high standards of personal and social morality meant that their lives were actually very tightly monitored and controlled, and their choices strictly limited. The inspectors, moral agents and schoolteachers were authorized to report the names of parents who did not send their children to the estate schools. These were run along the familiar and highly controversial evangelical lines. They were strictly scriptural and opened and closed with the singing of a psalm or hymn, the reading of a Bible chapter and a prayer. Lessons included the practicalities of arithmetic and needlework. But, while only Church of Ireland members were expected learn their church catechism, the reading and memorizing of biblical passages – expected of all children – posed a problem for Catholic families. The giving of premiums, to which the Catholic Church was so opposed, was forbidden, but the children's progress was recorded in a Judgment Book. Lying, indecent language, and non-attendance all resulted in expulsion. This could have a damaging effect on the welfare of the entire family, since not only the land agent but also Farnham himself, was kept personally informed of the behaviour of all on his estate. The whole issue of parental responsibility was thus given practical and immediate relevance.

Outside the schoolhouse too, the behaviour of all family members was expected to comply with the landlord's religious convictions. Any tenant charged with illicit distillation for example, was assured of immediate eviction. The singing of bawdy ballads was discouraged, and psalms were taught in the schools in a direct attempt to replace them. Parents were advised to keep their children from such vices as swearing, gambling and dancing, in their own interests of course, for

> Upon these points above all others will the favour and regard of their landlord depend, as upon the soundness of a man's religious and moral principles alone can a confidence be placed in his faithful discharge of his social and relative duties.[14]

The whole system seemed designed to erode traditional rural folk culture and replace it with an alternative set of values. It indicates too how evangelical Protestantism and social and economic progress were inextricably linked in the minds of its promoters, in the same way as Irish Catholic culture was associated with backwardness and inefficiency.

However, we should be aware that there were several different reasons behind this type of estate management. There was, firstly, a practical side to such paternalism. It can be seen as part of a more general overhaul of methods of estate management, which was one aspect of a process of improvement already in progress on Irish farms by the late 1820s. Concern with the consolidation of holdings and the implementation of a more streamlined and efficient system of management was entirely reconcilable with the new 'moral order'.[15] However, a study of the Manchester estate in County Armagh, where a similar system was introduced in 1833, revealed that more tenants were dispossessed for offences against the landlord's moral code than for non-payment of rent.[16] *The Devon Commission of Enquiry into the Occupation of Land in Ireland in 1844* also heard of the overriding importance of such considerations.[17] The influence which individual landlords could thus exercise over the daily lives of their tenantry was considerable.

Aristocratic landlords such as Farnham, Lord Roden in County Down, and Mandeville in Armagh, saw themselves as both political and religious leaders, in their local communities as well as at national level, and their small numbers belie the real significance of their influence. Marital connections and social contacts with evangelical and political leaders in England, along with the sheer size of their holdings, gave them a disproportionately strong influence in county and provincial society.[18] The bond between landlord and tenant was significantly strengthened by the personalizing of estate management, and the obvious temporal advantages to be gained by conforming to the landlord's expectations. This relationship was further strengthened by landed leadership of local Orange movements. Where the tenantry was mostly Catholic, however, the system of 'moral management' had major political and religious ramifications.

It is important to understand the distinctive characteristics of the locality and the tensions to which they gave rise. A rapid increase in the population had served to reinforce existing social and political tensions, with numbers rising from over 195,000 in 1821 to almost a quarter of a million twenty years later. It was an area in which both Catholic and Protestant religious leaders were concerned to increase their influence.

To further understand the intense religious rivalry which developed in Cavan, we need to be aware of the relative strengths of the religious institutions at this time. Particularly significant was the dynamic evangelical movement within Protestantism which had been gathering strength from the late eighteenth century.[19] Stressing the importance of personal conversion and individual salvation, British and Irish evangelicals had, from the early nineteenth century, focused their missionary zeal on the 'heathen' Catholics of Ireland. In a period of intensive activity, the bible was translated into Irish and widely disseminated throughout Catholic areas. At the same time, a range of religious societies set up schools to teach the bible, again in Irish and again targeting the Catholic peasantry. The London Hibernian Society and the Irish Society were the most numerous, vocal and controversial of these agencies, but there were many others. As Bishop Doyle remarked,

> There were not as many verse-makers in Rome in the days of Horace, as there are writers and speakers on education now-a-days in a single assembly of ladies and gentlemen in Ireland.[20]

Apart from – and indeed inseparable from - the strength of their own passionate religious convictions, evangelicals on the ground in Ireland were extremely anxious about the considerable progress which Catholicism there had been making since the end of the Penal era. That progress could be visibly monitored in the steady increase in the numbers of local clergy and in the new stone-built chapels which were emerging in many towns. That Catholics were also increasing in confidence was evident from the widespread popular support for Daniel O'Connell's Catholic Association, with most of the priests in the area involved in the collection of the association's penny a month 'rent' in aid of the campaign for Catholic Emancipation, which was achieved in 1829.[21]

In addition to their proselytizing or missionary activities, Protestant evangelical preachers also attacked Catholic theology, challenging the Catholic clergy about the very basis of their religion. To this end, the Reformation Society held a series of public meetings in the late 1820s, in both the north and south of the country. The aim, it was claimed, was 'to promote a spirit of religious enquiry' among Roman Catholics by engaging clergy from both traditions in debates over disputed doctrines. These emotive, angry, theological disputes were given huge media attention, and did much to increase local tensions.[22] The more 'respectable' clergy on both sides of the religious divide refused to engage in such public displays, and were highly critical of the 'fanatical', extreme and vulgar nature of these 'exhibitions'. The debate over conversions in County Cavan fed into this wider arena of controversy.

It is difficult too, to separate out the religious from the political aspects of these disputes. Evangelical landlords were particularly sensitive to the political tensions arising from O'Connell's popularity in the area. Landlords such as Farnham feared they were losing their political influence, a concern that seemed justifiable during the 1826 election campaign when many of the peasantry refused to support their landlord's nominee.[23] Such a situation reminded the ascendancy of its vulnerability in a country with a large Catholic majority, and the tensions were particularly strongly felt in border areas where the mix of religious allegiance introduced an element of competition into many aspects of life. Therefore it was not surprising that Protestant landlords sought a variety of means by which to exercise control, and assert their common interests with their tenantry.

A range of conflicting interests were at play in the area, which can be briefly summarized as follows:

Evangelical landlords
- Improved system of estate management
- Benevolent paternalism
- Political leadership
- Deep religious conviction
- [Religious and political vulnerability]

Catholic church
- Catholic progress
- Protecting their flock
- Religious conviction
- Political leadership
- [Sense of history and current movement for reform]

Tenantry
- Improving their homes
- Forging tighter relationship with landlord
- Protecting themselves
- Religious conviction
- Pragmatism
- [Under pressure of competing influences]

The actual statistics at the heart of the dispute are virtually impossible to verify. Each side had too much to gain, or to lose, for us to rely on their accuracy. The 'Second Reformation' was itself short-lived. Despite early optimism, the conversion of the Catholic population was eventually recognized as an unrealistic goal. Apart from the establishment of missionary 'colonies' in the west of Ireland in the 1830s and 40s, the attention of Protestant evangelicals became much more focused on the rejuvenation of religion within their own communities. The 'Great Awakening' of 1859 provides the best evidence of the religious strength of this movement, energizing the Protestant faithful and bypassing the Catholic population altogether.[24] In political terms, with the passing of Catholic Emancipation, and in direct relation to the growing sense of solidarity and purpose amongst the Catholic population, Protestantism became increasingly defensive. Ironically, it is undoubtedly the case that evangelical Protestants played a role in helping to raise Catholic religious consciousness. Their persistent and vehement public denunciations occasioned a vigorous defence of the Roman Catholic Church and its clergy, and a clearer exposition of its particular doctrines.

How then should we conclude? Research involves discovery, analysis, cross-reference and interpretation, and any conclusion reached must reflect the complexities of human experience, and the intricate, often competing, entanglements of social, political, religious and personal perspectives. After all, if problems such as that in Cavan in the 1820s were really simple black and white or orange and green affairs, then we would surely not still be facing the consequences of religious and political division at the beginning of the twenty-first century. If we have reached a clearer understanding of at least some of the multiple influences and pressures involved, then perhaps this, rather than a clear-cut definitive pronouncement on the rights and wrongs of the situation, is a valid and helpful historical exercise.

Notes and references

1 For a fuller account of the context of these controversies see, D Bowen, *The Protestant Crusade in Ireland 1800-1870* (Dublin 1978); D N Hempton and Myrtle Hill, *Evangelical Protestantism in Ulster Society 1740-1890* (London 1992).

2 Indeed, with an estate extending over several baronies, the Farnhams were the largest land proprietors in the country; Jacqueline Breiden, 'Tenant Applications to Lord Farnham, County Cavan 1832-60", in *Breifne*, Journal of Cumann Seanchais Bhreifne, Vol. ix, No. 36 (2000), pp173-224

3 Lord Farnham, *The Substance of a Speech delivered by the Rt. Hon, the Lord Farnham at a Meeting held in Cavan, on Friday, 20 January, 1828, for the Purpose of Promoting the Reformation in Ireland* (Dublin 1828).

4 Donal Kerr, 'James Browne, Bishop of Kilmore 1829-65, in *Breifne*, Journal of Cumann Seanchais Bhreifne, Vol. vi, No. 22, pp109-54, p123.

5 W J Fitzpatrick, *The life, times and correspondence of the Right Reverend Doctor Doyle*, ii (1890).

6 G Ensor, *Letters Showing the Inutility and the Absurdity of what is rather fantastically termed 'the New Reformation'* (Dublin 1828).

7 Ibid.

8 Farnham, *The substance of a speech...* op.cit.

9 J Madden, *Farnham Hall of The Second Reformation in Ireland: A Poem (Dublin 1827).*

10 *A Statement of the Management if the Farnham Estates* (Dublin 1830).

11 'Drivers' were the men paid to visit the tenantry in order to collect arrears. Their authority to impound livestock etc., and their exploitation of the situation in their own interests - for example, by charging extra fees for the release of stock - made them highly unpopular figures.

12 J R R Wright, ' An evangelical estate, c1800-1825; the influence on the Manchester estate, County Armagh, with particular references to the moral agencies of W Loftie and H Porter', PhD thesis, Northern Ireland Polytechnic, 1982. Wright points out that the term 'moral agent' was new, and finds no evidence of its use in England.

13 C S Stamford, *Memoir of the Late Reverend W H Krause* (Dublin 1854).

14 *A Statement of the Management of the Farnham Estates*, op.cit.

15 J S Donnelly, *Landlord and Tenant in Nineteenth-Century Ireland* (Dublin 1973), pp22-3.

16 Wright, 'An evangelical estate', op. cit.

17 *The Devon Commission of Enquiry into the Occupation of Land in ireland in 1844.*

18 I M Heihir, 'New Lights and old enemies, the Second Reformation and the Catholics of Ireland, 1800-1835', MA thesis, University of Winsconsin, 1983.

19 Myrtle Hill, 'Evangelicalism and the Churches in Ulster Society,1770-1850', PhD thesis, Queen's University Belfast, 1987.

20 J.K.L., *Letters on the State of Ireland* (Dublin 1825), p119.

21 Kerr, 'James Browne'. op. cit., p121.

22 Gideon Ouseley, *Old Christianity Defended* (Dublin 1820); Anon., *Appeal to members of the church of Rome residing in Randalstown and its vicinity*, 2nd edtn (Belfast 1827); Anon., *Protestants' Reasons for Not Worshipping Saints and Images* (Dublin 1827); Anon., *Authentic Report of the Discussions at Downpatrick* (Belfast 1829); Anon, *Authentic Report of the Discussion of Derry Between Six Roman Catholic Priests and Six Church of ireland Clergy* (Dublin 1828).

23 Farnham papers, Ms. 18602-30, National Library of Ireland.

24 Myrtle Hill, 'Ulster Awakened? the '59 Revival Reconsidered', in *The Journal of Ecclesiastical History*, Vol.41, No.3, July 1990, pp443-62.

Building bridges on the Border

Jack Johnston

I firmly believe that local history can be an instrument of reconciliation and can be used to build bridges between the various traditions in our country. I say this to you out of my own experience of working along the border here for more than twenty-five years. My conviction is based primarily on three areas of direct personal participation. Firstly, I was the voluntary Secretary of Clogher Historical Society for eighteen years. Secondly, within the last ten years I have been a project organiser for the Workers' Educational Association. And thirdly I presently, among other things, work for the Border Counties History Collective.

Clogher Historical Society, as many of you know, is one of the largest historical societies in Ireland. It has over 800 members and is based on the diocese. It is a cross-border institution in its own right with almost half of its territory in Northern Ireland - in Fermanagh and Tyrone - and the other half in the Republic of Ireland – largely in County Monaghan. It does today substantially represent our two main religious traditions in its membership, although this was not always the case.

The Society was founded in 1952 under the patronage of Bishop O'Callaghan and in its early years it was steered very much by a number of his Catholic clergy. They did commendable research into the early history of the diocese and into the antiquities of the area, publishing their work in the *Clogher Record*. It was pioneering work at the time, but had a fairly narrow base.

I felt that this good work could be widened to accommodate the story of another tradition as well. After I became Secretary in 1979 I began to develop this. There were others who shared my view, of whom Theo McMahon, the editor of the *Clogher Record* was one. Gradually we changed the perspective by broadening the content of the journal and introducing alterations to the programme.

In the early days the Society's annual general meetings and dinners were always held in Clones. This policy changed to alternate these events north and south, to hotels and schools in other centres of the diocese like Enniskillen, Ballybay, Lisnaskea, and Monaghan. This was not simply for the sake of trivial variety. We were asking our members to cross a border each year – a border on and around which there were a lot of tensions and difficulties at the time.

We then began choosing our president each year from north and south in turn. When I came to revive the coach outing in the late 1980s we again tried to bring people each way in turn. There were forays to the Boyne valley (1990), to Downpatrick and Inch (1991), to Dublin (1992), Armagh (1993), Foxford (1994), Gracehill (1995), and Boyle (1996). It soon proved to be a productive exercise in developing cross border links.

This idea of running alternating outings is also part of my current work with the Border Counties History Collective which has its office in Blacklion, County Cavan. Here the constituency is not the diocese of Clogher but the counties of Cavan, Leitrim, Fermanagh and Sligo. Two field trips stand out. We visited Killala in 1998 for the bi-centenary of the Humbert landing and I recall having with us some Fermanagh people who had never been in Connaught before. A few months later we had a trip from Blacklion to the Public Record Office and had with us some Sligonians who had never before been to Belfast. These outings nearly always had a meal planned for the homeward journey. There was more bridge building done here than any seminar could achieve.

The choice of venue is important if you are to make events accessible to all. The WEA were keen to make venues inclusive. Most halls had some tag or baggage with them and to get a class off the ground it was important to begin in a place that was clearly perceived to be 'neutral' like the local library. One group could find nothing 'neutral' and began by using the two schools on alternate months. Significantly, once the class was up and running the place of meeting became much less important.

C
o
Cooneen
n
i
a
n

This idea of the perception of place posed another difficulty for me with one group who were producing a publication. It was a good 'mixed' history group who had up to now worked easily together. The difficulty was that there were two ways of spelling the district's name. It was spelt as Cooneen by the Protestants and Coonian by the Roman Catholics. (I don't know how the poltergeist spelled it!)[1] How was this to be resolved when it came to the front cover of their book? After some heart searching we arrived at a formula which pleased them all and I am delighted to tell you that the idea was still being used on a dance ticket two years later.

The Border Counties History Collective, which has been operating now for over four years, is funded through the Peace and Reconciliation programme administered by Co-operation Ireland. Its main aim is to bring people and groups together through shared interest in local history. It is a network of twenty-three history societies on both sides of the border. The preamble to our first Annual Report highlights this thrust at peace building:

> The work of the Collective is rooted in the conviction that local history can help reconcile identities, create relationships and celebrate unique ways of life and culture.

We have tried to pursue this agenda in a number of ways. It has been important to select topics that will attract the widest possible audience in subjects that pose no threat to a productive discussion and analysis. We have had talks and lectures on surnames, railways, maps and map makers, genealogy and recently on the history of Co-operativism. Perhaps the time is not far off when we can be more adventurous and address areas with a more focused agenda. Having established the bridgehead of trust we are hoping to move on to some aspects of religious history. In fact our next talk is fairly unique in some ways. It is on the origins of Methodism in County Leitrim, but the speaker is not only a distinguished Leitrim historian but also a Roman Catholic priest.

The Collective's work as a network of local history groups is all about building trust and confidence within the realms of local studies and one of our most successful seminars has been on getting local history into print.

This brings me to local history publishing. There has been much good work done along the border in recent years that is a celebration of all the traditions in an area. Thankfully we have moved away from the narrow parish histories of fifty years ago that completely ignored 'the other side'. Among the best recent histories by individuals are *Irvinestown through the years* (Breege McCusker), and *Garrison – a Frontier for 2000 years* (Pat McGuinness), while groups in Ballygawley, Killinagh and Eskra have produced excellent inclusive documentaries of particular areas.

One of the finest of our local histories in recent years has been the monumental work on Ballybay by the Murnane brothers, James and Peadar. Their book *At the Ford of the Birches* – supported by the Ulster Local History Trust – is a high quality hardback of 670 pages which casts an inclusive net over all aspects of its area. Here there is wide inclusivity of all traditions and one chapter running to twenty-five pages fully documents the district's Freemasons, Hibernians, Foresters and Orangemen. We need to encourage authors who take inclusivity on board for they are bridge builders at the real grass roots of local history.

One of the Collective's services to local history groups is to help them with their publications. I have always emphasised that their texts should be free from bias and from the emotive word, or from anything that leaves people unjustifiably uncomfortable or distanced from the account. We need to explore the diversity of all communities and to relate it as openly and as evenly as we can.

Many years ago I remember reading Dr R B McDowell's biography of Mrs Green, the early twentieth century Irish historian. It was a fine book about a fine woman in stirring times. McDowell's title and subtitle was *Alice Stopford Green – A passionate historian*. Perhaps time has moved on. Today it has been my concern to produce a new breed along the border, here – a breed of dispassionate historians.

Note

1 Cooneen/Coonian, County Fermanagh, was the scene of one of modern Ireland's most celebrated hauntings.

Notes on contributors

John Bradley: vice-chairman of the Federation for Ulster Local Studies and a former teacher working at the Ulster American Folk Park, Omagh, County Tyrone.

Patricia Donlon: current chairman of the Education and Awareness Committee of the Heritage Council, Arnold Graves Scholar at the Dublin Institute of Technology, member of the Royal Irish Academy and former director of the National Library of Ireland.

Terence Dooley: historian and author whose most recent book is *The Decline of the Big House in Ireland*.

Patrick J Duffy: Professor of Geography at Maynooth College, National University of Ireland.

Seamus Heaney: poet; Patron of the Ulster Local History Trust.

Myrtle Hill: historian, trustee of the Ulster Local History Trust, and head of the Department of Women's Studies, Queen's University, Belfast.

Jack Johnston: farmer and historian who has served as secretary of the Clogher Historical Society and chairman of both the Federation for Ulster Local Studies and the Ulster Local History Trust.

John Lynch: historian, and lecturer in the Institute of Lifelong Learning at Queen's University, Belfast, where he is also convenor of the Certificate in Local Studies.

Linda McKenna: Community Education Officer at Down County Museum, Downpatrick.

Proinnsíos Ó Duigneáin: teacher in Manorhamilton, County Leitrim, and managing director of Drumlin Publications.

Edward O'Kane: lecturer at the Letterkenny Institute of Technology and a Past President of the County Donegal Historical Society.

Brian S Turner: museums and heritage consultant, trustee of the Ulster Local History Trust, founding Director of Down County Museum and former secretary of the Federation for Ulster Local Studies.

Aidan Walsh: museums and heritage consultant; first Curator of Monaghan County Museum, and former Director of the Northern Ireland Museums Council.

Registered conference participants

Adams, Rosemary, Clogher, co.Tyrone
Adams, Wilson, Clogher, co. Tyrone
Aghakillymaude Mummers, co. Fermanagh
Beattie, Mary, Belfast
Black, Lynn, Ballymena, co. Antrim
Bradley, John, West Tyrone Historical Society
Brand, Gordon, Enniskillen, co. Fermanagh
Brennan, Frank, Dublin
Brown, June, Clogher Historical Society
Callaghan, Jimmy, Roslea Heritage Centre, co. Fermanagh
Canning, Joe, Armagh
Cartwright, Cyril, Belfast
Cartwright, Margaret, Belfast
Cassidy, Patrick, Cootehill, co. Cavan
Clarke, Michael, Irvinestown, co. Fermanagh
Clarke, Patrick, Castlewellan, co. Down
Cleary, Bronagh, Fermanagh County Museum
Corcoran, Doreen, Ulster Local History Trust
Cowan, Roger, Annahagh, co. Monaghan
Crawford, Joe, Clogher Historical Society
Cunningham, Mary, Ballinode, co. Monaghan
Cunningham, Vincent, Newtownabbey, co. Antrim
Davison, Robert, Kircubbin, co. Down
Dempsey, Mairead, Dublin
Dinsmore, Nuala, Kilkerley, co. Louth
Donlon, Dr Patricia, Heritage Council
Donnan, Dr Hastings, Queen's University, Belfast
Dooley, Terence, Bray, co. Wicklow
Dudman, Moyra, Belfast
Duke, Pam, Queen's University, Belfast
Duffey, M J, Aughnacloy, co. Tyrone
Duffy, Most Reverend Dr Joseph, Monaghan
Duffy, Professor Patrick, National University of Ireland, Maynooth
Ennis, T P, Carrickaboy, co. Cavan
Eyben, Karen, Duncrun Cultural Initiative
Fawcett, Basil, Enniskillen, co. Fermanagh
Flood, James, Armagh
Flood, Mary, Paulstown, co. Kilkenny
Gildea, Seamus, Kilraine, co. Donegal
Gillespie, Dr Raymond, National University of Ireland, Maynooth
Gilsenan, Rev Michael, Carrickmacross, co. Monaghan
Grosse, M E, Clogher, co. Tyrone
Grosse, P S, Clogher, co. Tyrone
Guy, Maisie, Enniskillen, co. Fermanagh
Hagan, Felix, Dungannon, co. Tyrone
Hamilton, Mary, Tempo Historical Society, co. Fermanagh

Hammond, David, Flying Fox Films, Belfast
Hannon, Joan, Cootehill, co. Cavan
Harvey, Stephen, Ballyclare, co. Antrim
Heaney, Breda, Aughnacloy, co. Tyrone
Heaney, Bridín, Aughnacloy, co. Tyrone
Heaney, Professor Seamus, Patron of the Ulster Local History Trust
Herbert, Vicky, Lisnaskea, co. Fermanagh
Hill, Dr. Myrtle, Ulster Local History Trust

Holland, Patrick, Carrickmacross, co. Monaghan
Hughes, Ita, Carrickmacross, co. Monaghan
Johnston, Audrey, Clogher, co. Tyrone
Johnston, Donal, Dundalk, co. Louth
Johnston, Jack, Ulster Local History Trust
Keaney, Maura, Belcoo, co. Fermanagh
Keaney, Maureen, Manorhamilton, co. Leitrim
Kelly, Eileen, Sligo
Kelly, Patrick, Sligo
Kennedy, Fergus, Longford County Arts Office
Kingston, Ann, Montrath, co. Laois
Knight, George, Clones, co. Monaghan
Lunny, Sean, Enniskillen, co. Fermanagh
Lynch, Dr John, Queen's University, Belfast
MacArthur, Brigid M, Letterkenny, co. Donegal
MacArthur, Colan W P, Letterkenny, co. Donegal
McCabe, Dermot, Clones, co. Tyrone
McCaffrey, Mary, Fivemiletown, co. Tyrone
McCaffrey, Oliver, Roslea Heritage Centre
McCluskey, Seamus, Emyvale, co. Monaghan
McCormick, Colin, Enniskillen, co. Fermanagh
MacDonaill, Dr Donal, Trinity College, Dublin
McElgunn, Dolores, Cavan
McElgunn, Sean, Cavan
McGauran, Sean, Manorhamilton, co. Leitrim
McGinty, Annie, Roslea Heritage Centre

Pat Donlon (left) of the Heritage Council with Myrtle Hill (centre) and Helen Turner from the Ulster Local History Trust.

Michelle McGoff computing.

McGoff, Michelle, Clogher Historical Society
McGovern, Concepta, County Cavan Heritage & Genealogical Society
McGrady, Colette, Downpatrick, co. Down
McGrady, Malachy, Ulster Local History Trust
McGrath, Niamh, Ballyhaise Agricultural College, co. Cavan
McGuire, Peter, Duncrun Cultural Initiative
McKenna, Eileen, Scotstown, co. Monaghan
McKenna, Linda, Down County Museum
McKenna, Mary, JP, Clogher, co. Tyrone
McKevitt, Jane, Dublin
MacKiernan, Most Rev Dr Francis, Cavan
MacMahon, Theo, Ulster Local History Trust
McMahon, Michael, Heritage Council
McManus, Eugene, Enniskillen, co. Fermanagh
McManus, Marianne, Enniskillen, co. Fermanagh
McNally, Catherine, County Cavan Heritage & Genealogical Society
McPhillips, Michael, Newtownbutler, co. Fermanagh
Macklin, Celestine, Monaghan
Macklin, Mary, Monaghan
Maguire, Bridget, Brookborough, co. Fermanagh
Maguire, Dermot, Newtownbutler, co. Fermanagh
Maguire, Dr M E, Enniskillen, co. Fermanagh
Malley, Annesley, Ulster Local History Trust
Martin, Neil, Flying Fox Films, Belfast
Maxwell, Marion, Enniskillen, co. Fermanagh
Moen, Phyllis, Clontibret, co. Monaghan
Montgomery, George, Ballybay, co. Monaghan
Montgomery, Nixon, Ballybay, co. Monaghan
Montgomery, Norah, Armagh
Montgomery, Roberta, Armagh
Moore, Ruth, Fermanagh District Council
Mullin, Larry, Sligo
Murphy, Jim, Monaghan
Murphy, Mary, Warrenpoint, co. Down
Murphy, Sheila, Monaghan

Nash, Dr Catherine, University of London
Nolan, Jim, Enniskillen, co. Fermanagh
Nolan, Rev Sean, Emyvale, co. Monaghan
Nugent, Angela, Warrenpoint, co. Down
Ó Baoighill, Padraig, Monaghan
O'Brien, Pat, Ballygawley, co. Sligo
Ó Dincin, Alfai, Monaghan
Ó Dincin, Filimine, Monaghan
O'Donnell, Mary, Enniskillen, co. Fermanagh
Ó Duigneáin, Proinnsíos, Manorhamilton, co. Leitrim
O'Ferrall, Fergus, Dublin
O'Kane, Eddie, County Donegal Historical Society
Ó Luana, Seosamh, Cloghereragh, co. Sligo

O'Neill, Hugh, Larne, co. Antrim
O'Neill, Maire, Clogher Historical Society
O'Reilly, Brid, Ballyconnell, co. Cavan
O'Reilly, Eugene, Ballyconnell, co. Cavan
O'Reilly, Margaret, Derrycramph, co. Cavan
O'Reilly, Rita, Monaghan
Pollak, Dr Andy, Centre for Cross Border Studies, Armagh
Prunty, Dr Jacinta, National University of Ireland, Maynooth

Seosamh Ó Luana among the crowd.

Reihill, John James, Inishcorkish, co. Fermanagh
Robinson, Hazel, Enniskillen, co. Fermanagh
Robinson, Sam, Enniskillen, co. Fermanagh
Rooney, Brendan, Glencar, co. Sligo
Ross, Noel, Dundalk, co. Louth
Scarlett, Duncan, Lisburn, co. Antrim
Skeath, Henry, Monaghan
Smyth, Eileen, Roslea Heritage Centre, co. Fermanagh
Steele, J Thompson, Belfast
Steele, Mrs, Belfast
Steenson, Elizabeth, Ballybay, co. Monaghan
Steenson, Graham, Ballybay, co. Monaghan
Smyth, Professor William, Heritage Council
Sullivan, Tom, County Cavan Heritage & Genealogical Society
Swan, Wendy, Derrycramph, co. Cavan
Tannian, Bridie, Enniskillen, co. Fermanagh
Timoney, Una, Omagh, co. Tyrone
Trainor, Dr Brian, Ulster Historical Foundation
Turner, Dr Brian, Ulster Local History Trust
Turner, Helen, Ulster Local History Trust
Walsh, Aidan, Castlepollard, co. Westmeath
Wilson, Henry, Moira, co. Down

The Heritage Council

The Heritage Council was established in the Irish Republic under the Heritage Act, 1995. It is an independent body which has a statutory responsibility pursuant to section 6 of the Act, "to propose policies and priorities for the identification, protection, preservation and enhancement of the national heritage". The Council's chairman and sixteen members are appointed by the Minister for Arts, Heritage, Gaeltacht and the Islands, determining policy for the organisation and devising the organisational programme.

National heritage is defined in the Act as including:

- Monuments
- Archaeological objects
- Heritage objects
- Architectural heritage
- Flora
- Fauna
- Wildlife habitats
- Landscapes
- Seascapes
- Wrecks
- Geology
- Heritage gardens and parks
- Inland waterways

In particular, the Heritage Act, 1995, charges the Heritage Council with the responsibility to:

- promote interest, education, knowledge and pride in, and facilitate the appreciation and enjoyment of the national heritage;
- co-operate with other bodies in the promotion of its functions; and
- promote the co-ordination of all activities relating to its functions.

The Council has appointed fifteen professional and administrative staff, including a Chief Executive. The function of the staff is to conduct the day-to-day business of the Council and to provide it with expert policy advice.

Contact information:
By post:
The Heritage Council
Kilkenny

By electronic mail:
heritage@heritagecouncil.com

Web site:
www.heritagecouncil.ie

The Ulster Local History Trust

The Ulster Local History Trust is dedicated to raising standards and promoting innovation in the voluntary local history movement within the nine counties of Ulster.

Patron: Seamus Heaney

Trustees: Doreen Corcoran, John Cunningham, Cahal Dallat, David Harkness, Myrtle Hill, Jack Johnston, Patrick Loughrey, Malachy McGrady, Theo McMahon, Annesley Malley, Lord O'Neill, Brian Turner.

The Trust is an independent voluntary and charitable body established by the Federation for Ulster Local Studies to help raise the standard of local historical work, particularly among voluntary groups, and to assert its relevance in our society. In the last decade it has supported over 100 local history projects.

The Trust has the nine counties of Ulster as its area of primary concern and this deliberate policy is intended to emphasise both inclusiveness and a willingness to recognise that difference can be respected and welcomed rather than feared. The trustees believe that the study of our history on a human scale carries not only personal interest for the individual, but can get to the heart of many of the questions which challenge our sense of identity and cultural confidence in the modern world.

Contact Information:

By post:

Ulster Local History Trust

PO Box 900

Downpatrick

County Down BT30 6EF

By electronic mail:

ulht@ulht.org

Web site:

www.ulht.org

Index